From The Author WHO BROUGHT YOU **LIFE IS ABOUT CHOICES!!!**

Taking YOUR LIFE UP A NOTCH

"THE SKY IS THE LIMIT FOR YOU"

ERNEST D. SULLIVAN

WWW.MCCLUREPUBLISHING.COM

Taking Your Life UP A Notch

"The Sky Is The Limit For YOU!"

By Ernest D. Sullivan

Copyright @ 2017 Ernest Devon Sullivan

All rights reserved. No Part of this publication may be reproduced or transmitted in any form or by any means, with the exception of brief quotes for purposes of review, without the written permission of the author.

Printed in the United States of America

Cover Design by

Macro Publishing Co.

ISBN: 978-0-9915335-1-0

To order additional copies, log on to
www.mcclurepublishing.com
800-659-4908

"My life has meaning because I choose not to quit."
-Ernest D. Sullivan-

Dedicated To

My Children

Dominique Mechelle Sullivan

Danisha Lenae Sullivan

Ilias Loren Sullivan

&

Men, Women, the Homeless,

Individuals in School, Prisons, Military, and

Individuals who know that the
SKY IS THE LIMIT!!!!!

ACKNOWLEDGEMENTS

This book came to be, in part, through individuals in my family---friends, and individuals who are on the verge of success. I have come across many successful and unsuccessful people in my life and I have to say they both impacted my life and have inspired this book.

My mother Bobbie Jean Travis, my grandmother Lillie Mae Sullivan (1927-1984) and my granddad James Sullivan (1920-1990) gave me some invaluable advice to be all that I can be and more. I would like to give thanks to my Pastor Dr. Randolph Howard who feed me spiritually. My Pastor empowers me, encourages me, and embraces my ministry. Bishop T.D. Jakes inspires me because listening to his sermons on a regular basis is often the affirmation I need to live my passion. Anyone who knows me understand that family is very important to me.

I have a typical family that exudes many different personalities, but I love each and every one of them. My aunt Shirley is special because she has never changed and has always treated me with love. My aunt Harriet is my second mother because she always calls and checks on me. My aunt Laverne was my baby, because she looked to me for many things. My aunt Geraldine is the youngest and her energy ignites me. My uncle Michael Sullivan (aka) Mickey is unique but his love for his family will never be overlooked. My deceased uncle James "Slim" Sullivan (1953-2007) was my friend and he taught me a lot of things. My uncle James Siler he taught me how to understand life. In addition, my uncle Wayne Young, James Sylvester and Claude Smith who also played a valuable part in my development as a man.

I salute each of you and I want the world to know that family is the best gift any person can have. You all made me proud. I want you to give me an opportunity to make you proud as well.

Love Ernest D. Sullivan

Table OF Contents

Acknowledgements

Introduction

Chapter 1 15
Are you on Ground Zero?

Chapter 2 27
Are You Looking for Fame?

Chapter 3 43
Do YOU have the POWER?

Chapter 4 53
Will YOU follow your Heart?

Chapter 5 65
Are you ready for your MISSION?

Chapter 6 73
Have you decided to Take Your Life up a Notch?

Chapter 7 85
What Price are You willing to Pay?

Chapter 8 95
Do You Know Where you are headed?

Chapter 9..**105**
Are You Ready to Make It Happen?

Chapter 10 ....**115**
The Sky is the Limit for YOU!

The Motivating Moments

10 Reasons Why You.........

Notes To Start Your Engine

Partnerships & Sponsorships

About the Author

Special Thanks

INTRODUCTION

Taking Your Life Up A Notch

Does your life feel like you are living a "bad dream?" Are you afraid to take control of your life and take it up a Notch or Two? What is stopping you from taking control of the remote starter that has been hard-wired inside of you? Your next dream will become a reality if you think it first, speak it into your life, and then act on it. You are on the verge of the greatest miracle that is about to take over your life. Can you see success in your future?

I would like to take you on a journey traveling on a one-way ticket to success. This book will challenge some people's way of thinking because most people do not travel by themselves. I am encouraging you to start making preparations for what is to come in your life. You need to get your expensive luggage pack with the right stuff inside. Stuff like ambitions, goals, dreams, and most importantly your desires to be great. You do not have another wasted moment to get ready.

The time is now and positioning yourself right now for success is the key to your success. When was the last time you achieved a goal? How did it make you feel? Well your next achievement will propel you to the next level. Are you ready?

Identify Your Purpose no matter what it is that has control over your life, you cannot live unless you identify your purpose. You can start by recognizing what it is that you enjoy and get fulfillment from. You know that good feeling you feel inside and no one but you can get the victory from doing it. For example, "It's like jumping in a swimming pool with a black wet suit on, and then getting out and wetting yourself." I know what you are thinking, THAT'S NASTY! Just think about it, you will get a warm feeling and no one else will notice or feel it but you.

Never allow your purpose to be lost because you are holding on to something or someone who is holding you back. The biggest mistake you can make is to place your goals and dreams aside trying to satisfy others. Others may include your parents, spouse, family, friends, boyfriends, girlfriends and/or boss. For clarity, these are only individuals who are selfish enough to hold you back while they chase their dreams to potentially control your future. You have been armed with a great mind and the only way you can be denied finding your purpose will be because YOU chose not to use it.

There will come a time in your life that you must learn how to encourage yourself. When you feel like the world has turned its back on you that is when you must lean on the ROCK! Who was the last person to hug you? It may have been your mother, father, brother, sister, spouse, or even a friend but if not HUG YOURSELF! Sometimes finding out how much you love yourself will determine how much others will display love towards you.

Are you always fighting battles that are not yours and as a result the person(s) you were defending told you that you were wrong? I have learned that sometimes you can be right and wrong because of the way you handle a situation. It's time now to rise above situations and pursue your Purpose, and then The Sky Is The Limit For You. It's time to Take Your Life Up A Notch!

We will embrace why your Life Is Worth Living and how a S.H.I.F.T must occur in your life for you to reach your full potential. You will be challenged to change your current way of thinking so you can get on the express elevator to the top. You might be stuck on the first floor, but I am about to pump your head with enough fuel to boost you to the next level. You will board an aircraft and see the world from a new perspective because you are headed to your new address The Sky is the Limit Boulevard!

Are you ready to take your life out of Park and start DRIVING to the airport for your journey? This book will point you in the direction that your life is predestined for you to go. When you make it to your next destination you will be ready for the assignment. Your preparation to

Taking Your Life Up A Notch is the most critical aspect for you to reach the Sky.

The Sky Is The Limit For You because you will not let obstacles stop you from being successful. You are able to flourish in areas that others sink in. You will be equipped with your protective wet suit to absorb problems. Have you considered how you are going to reach for the sky? Did you know that your parachute will not open if you fall and never reach a high enough altitude? This book will give you steps, phases, elements, and ways on how to save yourself from falling once you start making your dreams happen. I am here to tell you that the Sky Is The Limit for you. Your time is now and if you want to Take Your Life Up A Notch, get ready to be motivated, challenged, and mentored for reaching heights that you have always dreamed about. Your new life starts now. The life you live now has put you in a position to make a choice to go further in life, then go further than that, or just stay where you are. You are a mover and a shaker, you need to keep moving forward or risk being caught by the idle-bug. Idle means, not moving, just staying where you are which is the recipe for a depress state of mind. You are a born leader and the leader inside you is ready to lead.

Do you realize that "It Is Your Turn Now?" You might ask, "My time for what?" I am so glad you asked. It's your time to reach higher and to prosper this year and years to come while on your Mission. When was the last time you told yourself that you are going to make your life better? I did not say need to make it better. There will be concepts to challenge your thoughts about wants and needs. You need to be successful, because wanting to be successful will not be enough to reach the heights that your life can achieve. The ultimate goal is to show you how to Make it Happen before you are successful, during the process, and once you make it to maintain a superior level of success.

This book will give you the confidence and courage to push yourself to the next level. What floor are you on? The elevator just closed so are you ready to Take Your Life Up a Notch? You just started moving on the elevator to success. What floor will you get off on? I will be waiting for you at the airport where you will begin your journey to Taking Your Life Up a Notch!

"Your success has been determined by the one person who matters, You."
-Ernest D. Sullivan-

Now it's time to get off on the top floor, let's get started because your life is worth living.

CHAPTER 1
Are you on Ground Zero?

"Non-cooperation with evil is a duty."
-Mahatma Gandhi-

Can you imagine waking up and seeing the world upside down? I mean when you wake up and look up all you see is the ground, and then when you look down you can see the sky. Wouldn't that be a shame to now be looking down on something you suppose to look up too? I am imagining a beautiful blue sky now at a person's feet and all they can do is now imagine and feel sorry for themselves. Then imagine looking up and all you have above you is the concrete ground that should be beneath you. Do you know that if a person just learn how to turn their imagination around to see the world from a better vantage point, life can get better? Life has a funny way of confusing the brain to think one way, but in reality it can be turned around when your thoughts change. Speaking from a person who have struggled a day or two with the possibility of not being successful, we can learn to shift our thoughts and prosper.

TAKING YOUR LIFE UP A NOTCH
"The Sky Is The Limit For You"

One of the worst feelings in the world is to feel like you are at the bottom and cannot find the strength to get up. I am here to tell you that you can get up. Are you ready to learn how to take your life up a notch? Life has not only thrown you a curve ball, but it has a way of striking a lot of people out. When was the last time you were encouraged to follow your dreams? Well on this day, I salute you and will offer the encouragement some people may need. Have you ever been the person that your spouse, family or friends lean on because they believe that you have the answer to the world problems? They probably never considered if you were experiencing any problems yourself. This chapter will be the only chapter that identifies the pitfalls that causes people to need to take their lives up a notch.

When you look at a homeless man or woman sleeping in the streets, what are your initial thoughts? For most people their thoughts are probably, "what a shame," what happened. I can tell you that most often if you have ever had a chance to talk to a homeless person they will say that it was other people, the world, their families, their job, or finally, themselves are the reasons for being homeless. I know it sounds like a list of not accepting full responsibilities for ones actions. I know a person should accept the choices that he or she has made that lead them to ground-zero. Nonetheless, can I get you to see the Freedom Tower? The beautiful designed building standing at 1,776', 1,792' square feet to the tip? Do you know where this building originated from, Ground-Zero. Not litigating the past of September 11, 2001 but I am here to tell you that things that hit ground-zero can and will soar high again. Can you imagine your life or someone you know hitting ground-zero and never attempting to get up? What would you say or call that person? Most will call them a bum, a failure, a free-loader, a drug addict, a loser, a thief, or even a nuisance. Why because they chose to stay down or because you and I did not choose to help pick them back up. I sincerely believe in rebuilding people when they have been broken down. I would like to see the new Freedom-You built from grown-zero because that is a design that cannot be imitated.

If your brand has been smeared, I just received a lifetime supply of smear removal, and I have more than enough to give it away to whoever needs it. This smear removal works on all people and the surfaces they lay down on. This is some life-changing removal that can take something old and make it new again. Does the Freedom-You need, needs a make-over? Some of our dispositions and make up looks old and smeared; I am asking you to embark on this journey with me to take your life up a notch. I need YOU to begin thinking of every excuse that you heard or used and say, "I am putting every excuse in a sealed lockbox." These are the excuses that you need to clean yourself up with before the smear removal can work. You know how we clean up an area before people see them, that's what I need you to do with the things that's holding a lot of you back. There are four areas in your body I will call "rooms" that need to be cleaned before you can take this trip.

- Room #1- *The room of pride* lives inside of many people including myself because it is something that we have strong convictions about. I am here to tell you that replacing pride with stride will change your life forever. So often we can miss our destination because we are traveling alone to a place we have never been. There is nothing wrong with seeking help, listening, realizing that you do not know it all sometimes. The worst thing any prideful person can say is I did it without the word **but** behind it. Sometimes the word **but** is necessary to eliminate the prideful thoughts that is inside of prideful people. Mr. and Mrs. Pride you are not looked upon favorably by the world's standards and you will find yourself at ground-zero if you do not commit to changing your ways. Oftentimes, people end up blocking their paths to success because they have to be right. Many people with pride are revengeful and they possess that, "I will show them," type of attitude. Pride can be tricky because it is closely associated with revenge. Start today because revenge sometimes takes a lifetime to fulfill, but setting aside pride can clean your slate.

- Room#2- *The room of hurt* that lives inside of many people has destroyed any chances of them ever having the ability to reverse the curse. This pain has lived inside of the person for so many years that without proper guidance most will die with it. Do you know of anyone who wants to die hurting? Well I was sent to tell you, not on my watch. The hurt that a person feels can be used in two ways and two ways only, a person can decide to let it stay or let it go. I want YOU to let it go because sometimes asking a question or giving a choice sometimes does not bring on the best response. Going on this journey is an opportunity and option for you to let it go. Hurting, hurts but letting it go releases you from the pain that you will not need on this journey. I have been hurt just like you many times but the one thing that will separate our hurt from other people's hurt is **Perseverance.** There is never a need for perseverance when things are going well in your life; we only need it activated when we are struggling through some things like finances, relationships, tests, and pain. If you have never had to persevere to reach a solution, you have been living a life many people could only fantasize about having. (Sorry) News flash I suggest that you pay your premium up on persevering because if you do not need it today you may need it in the future. So for any person that has experienced hurt, let it go because your preparation to take your life up a notch depends on it. Remember these words; let it go so that you can grow.

- Room#3- *The room of hating everybody* that you feel that was not there for you, can make a person start hating themselves. I do not know about you but as a young man it was hard for people that loved you to say they hated you and mean it. This new-age hatred appears easier for some individuals now to exhibit hate towards the people they love and quite naturally against people they do not. What happens to all people matters? The hate that a person bottles up is like the pressure that builds up in a steel pipe. People need to release the hate because if they do not it will cause a person to make a decision that cannot be corrected. Most people will not tell the truth about themselves, but I will share a story about myself. One day at a relative's house I got upset with my family and I went into the kitchen and I broke a glass. This was not an ordinary glass mind you, but a sentimental glass of my aunts. I was afraid of how my aunt would react and the first thing that came to my mind was to rectify my hatred at the time and say, **I'm Sorry**. Even though, I said that I was sorry I then realized that this was my family who loves me unconditionally, but that glass could not be put back together again. Therefore, when hate is involved in a person's heart, sometimes they can say or do things that cannot be fixed. Learn to love and stop hating because your hate towards another lives inside of who, YOU. We cannot replace hate with anything accept with forgiveness. Forgiving others is a sign of maturity. Maturity is needed for the direction you are headed and where you are going. Remember the sky is the limit.

- Room#4- *The room of life* that's buried inside of many people who are stuck on ground-zero dying inside. This is the room that only you can clean, I am here to help you clean out your pride room, hurt room, and your hating room, but for your Life-Room only you can clean out because it's yours. This room is most often the junkiest for some people because we place everything that we think we need in this room. I am about to share with you in reality some of the things that is a must in your Life-Room.

    o   You must have Faith

- You must have Passion
- You must have Desire
- You must have Opportunity
- You must have a higher power leading your thoughts.
- You must have a clean heart
- You must have a helping attitude
- You must have a support system
- You must have a plan

Sometimes we overcrowd this room trying to please everybody and excluding the main person that matters, ourselves. Did you notice that I did not include family as a must? I chose not to because Family should have their own room inside of a person's body. If you do not believe me I will prove it. Think of any couple that you can think of as successful in life. Can you now think about what that couple does to live and consider them as an example? I could have easily used a celebrity power couple, but I want you to envision you and your mate as an everyday power couple. These are the people who made a life for themselves so that they could support and assist their families. Most often when the couples are living their passion they are away from each other, but when they make their life great, they then come together as a family. I am not just talking about a spouse. It can be the coming together with children, parents, aunts, uncles, cousins, friends, partners etc.... So often, people attempt to compartmentalize a person's life based on where they come from. Yes, this includes their economic upbringing. Believe you will ultimately be viewed by the life **You** live not anyone else's. Your life has a meaning all by itself and no person can live it for you. Look at how many celebrities' children encounter unfair treatment because others see their parents' story inside of them instead of the person they were chosen to become. Do you want to live life with regrets? I know you do not, so make yourself proud and live your life to the fullest.

I understand that sometimes it seems like it's too much to handle but it's all in your perception. Changing your perception about where you are can become the start of where you are going. I am ready to show you how to take your life up a notch but I need YOU to fall in love with you before we start. I would always ask my family and friends these questions, how can a man fall out the bed, if he sleeps on the floor? I do not know the answer either, but I do know any person that lies down and refuses to get up may have chosen to give up. Do you know that there are people disable that still find a way to get up even when faced with a disadvantage that was dealt to them. Your cards can be reshuffled and dealt again, are you ready for your next chance to win?

I would like to share some quotes that will assist you while you are cleaning out your rooms.

- "The trick is to enjoy life. Don't wish away your days, waiting for better days ahead."
  -Marjorie Pay Hinckley-

- "The greats knew they were great before anyone else did."
  -Unknown-

- "Sometimes the obstacles that need removed from your life have names."
  -Unknown-

- "Never give up on something you can't go a day without thinking about, Your Life."
  -Ernest D. Sullivan-

- "I refuse to allow what I did, what I didn't do, or what I should've done, effect what I'm about to do."
  -Unknown-

Any life of foolishness is categorized as living for the moment instead of living for a purpose. You have cleaned out your rooms so now you are ready for the smear removal.

I want to first thank you for investing in your life. The instructions for using smear removal are written clear, but the process of applying will be outlined throughout the chapters to take you from Ground-Zero to the newest design made, **Freedom-You**. Whatever you do please do not allow your newly designed **Freedom-You** to get smeared again chasing something that have gotten some people to ground-zero in the first place. Taking your life up a notch is a calling on your life. Never forget cars get recalled often. This is when the manufacturers admit to making a mistake. In all cases they fix the problem for free. The information that I am giving is free as well. Let your journey begin.

CHAPTER 2
Are You Looking for Fame?

"Life is what happens while you're making your plans."
-Allen Saunders-

Have you ever had a friend that's only around when things are going good? In life we experience a multitude of highs and lows. I am here to explore the difference between a person being there for you or someone being there for something from you. We must be careful of who we allow in our circle of success. In many instances people that you thought were your friends were only placed in your life to push you into your destiny. Even if you decide to break the situationship off, always know that he/she played an intricate part in your growth. Believe it or not the person(s) that you spent the most time with has done you the biggest favor in the world. They helped you without you knowing. In one instance, they helped by assisting you with structuring your life that ultimately shapes your future. You now can develop a mission statement for your life that fulfills and explains the **Three**

P's. Your **Passion, Purpose,** and **Priorities** because these 3 P's will help you decipher which people are in your life for Fame and which are in your life to support your Mission. I did not say help with your mission because we cannot make our missions and dreams another person's reality. We are made and were made whole. We can only function with what's inside of us. Let's start with understanding what and how passion can help with your mission.

Passion is a noun, or **passion**; plural noun: this noun describes several aspects of how our emotions drive our thinking process.

1. Any powerful or compelling emotion or feeling, as love or hate;
2. Strong amorous feeling or desire; love; ardor;
3. Strong sexual desire, lust;
4. An instance or experience of strong love or sexual desire;
5. A person toward whom one feels strong love or sexual desire;
6. A strong or extravagant fondness, enthusiasm, or desire for anything your heart desires; and
7. The object of such a fondness or desire.

Have you identified what's your passion? Then you can develop a plan to start living and walking into your passion. What is the one thing that you will do, or love to do and you will do even if you did not get paid for it? When you identify that one thing, then you have found your passion? To find your passion is to live a life of success and not having to spend so many working hours to achieve it. I am not saying that your Passion does not require hard work, but it does include enjoying what you do.

The questions are, have you identified your passion? Have you identified the person(s) that will assist you with your passion? Have you researched how much money and time it will take to reach your full potential? Have you developed your plan of actions to achieve your goal? You will need to identify and answer these questions before you can live your passion. Please do not wait on somebody else to jumpstart your mission. You can start by getting connected with the people that can mentor you into greatness. Because in life you will not need fair-weathered family or friends, you will need die-hard genuine people in your life. Know the difference! You are equipped with many talents and gifts but do you know how to apply and utilize them? Here are **5L's** to help you bring your talents and gifts to the surface.

- **Learn** how to invest in yourself (this may require dedicating time for you and your passion). It may seem hard to do, but this is a requirement not a request. Every successful person made time for their greatness. The first step starts with you, take that step. When you start moving in the direction of your passion you will be amazed of the people who support you. You are ready now. There is no more time to be wasted, wishing you could live your dream. Now stretch out your arms and yawn because you have slept long enough on your passion. I want you to live effectively for years and years to come. Do me a favor from this day forward, read more, study more, and research more because that is what all the great people do.

- **List** all of your talents and gifts (write them down and post them where you can be reminded of them). This is important in the process because identifying what you do best will lead you to success. Your gift is unique and cannot be duplicated. I know, nothing is new under the sun, but there is only one you under the sun. Use your gifts and talents and show the world something different. Some people are resistant to change while others embrace uniqueness. Take your list and evaluate it yearly because by then it may be time to pull another gift out. Yes you have more than one gift. List your short-term goals, intermediate goals, and your long-term goals and watch how your life changes.

- **Look** for all resources that you will need (spend 3-6 months preparing for your passion). This is the research and development period. You must know what it takes to be successful. Remember, you do not have all the answers. The resources can be utilized to bridge the gap between using productive time versus wasted time. Learn all the strategies that are needed, ask questions, and even accept a lesser role to learn. Look for all innovative ways to live your dream.

- **Locate** all support groups that will be needed to fund your passion (You are a product; get someone to invest into your idea). I will start as your first supporter, now who else can you think of? Do you know that there are people who need to invest in others to fulfill their mission? Did you hear me, people and organizations set aside extra money to help others. In addition, do you know that an effective fundraiser can propel you to having enough to fund your mission? Believe me your job is not designed to fund your mission. Your vision is larger than your pay check. Remember that.

- **Leap** forward with your dream (now you are prepared to live your Passion). Do you know that most often there is something in front of you that you can stand on that will allow you to see your destiny? Your new view is putting you that much closer to what you have been dreaming about. This is the perfect time for you to achieve your goals. I want you to leap higher than you ever imagined because leaping is exciting. Take it out of your head, "What if I fall, Fail?" My answer remains simple, so. Leap again, and again, and again. Because this is your life and I heard this saying from people for a long time, "I have leaped over forward and backward to help someone else." Well now it's time to leap for **YOU!**

These 5L's will not catapult you from obscurity to notoriety but this is the blueprint to get you started toward your passion. But, if you are only looking for fame, then follow the status quo of hoping to luck up on ways to utilize your talents and gifts. On this journey, there will be many naysayers and doubters. Are you prepared for this test? These will be the individuals who attempt to discourage you and try to derail your quest to pursue your passion. They camouflage themselves sometimes in the forms of family, friends, significant others, co-workers, teachers, and most definitely your enemies. Ask yourself this, do you require a lot of validation? Because if you are built faithfully tough, then your answer should be, no, but if you are built without it you might break. Now is not the time to break and depend on others to validate you. Now is the time to surge forward with all your strength.

Let me encourage you further to start looking at your life coming together as a puzzle and as each piece is added, your life will become whole. Your talents and gifts are strong because that is what **Passion** entails. Passion cannot be hidden. Passion can be seen in the eyes of a person. I challenge you to dig deep down inside of your body and tell it to the world without talking. Do you have strong beliefs for the strong purpose that is on your life? Answering yes to the previous question will put one piece of the puzzle in place. Now, do you know your **Purpose**?

Purpose is a noun also that will describe the aspects of how your emotions will drive your thought process.

1. The reason for which something exists or is done, made, used, etc.
2. An intended or desired result; end; aim; goal.
3. Determination; resoluteness.
4. The subject in hand; the point at issue.
5. Practical result, effect, or advantage: to act to good purpose.

The purpose for your life is yours, not anyone else's. It all starts with you and only you. Look up the definition of your purpose and use it as a guide to get you to a level that you can reach and achieve. If your purpose means something to you, then it will mean something to others. We are entertained by many things, Television, Sporting Events, Entertainers, therefore, your purpose means equally as much. You possess something that this world needs to experience, unleash your purpose. Do you know what your purpose to this world is? I have developed a concept to assist you with your purpose. It's called H. E. L. P.

- **H**old on to your dream because once you deny it, it will abandon your thoughts of making it a reality. The two easiest words to ever say in this lifetime is, "I Quit." Do you know that dreams aren't meant to last forever? That's why you wake up because if you keep dreaming it will never become reality. Are you awake yet? Put your plan into action now.

- Elevate yourself higher by identifying all of your resources that will be needed to fulfill your purpose. This requires a few things often, an education, financing, and a purpose. Your purpose need to be lifted high enough for the purpose to reach its full meaning. Set high standards for your purpose because you are destined for success.

- **L**aughter is a universal language that is accepted across the world. You cannot develop a purpose that excludes others from witnessing it. It is also good for the soul. Make sure fun is included in your success because it's a requirement. Give people something to smile about every time they encounter your mission. I want you to be the reason that someone smiles each day.

- **P**ropose a new way to utilize an existing idea used before. Cell phones are being updated frequently, the remaking of movies, and brands are remade. People do same or similar things, but you have a gift to do it differently. Make your ideas a new trend. Therefore, your personal touch will bring your purpose into fruition. I believe you can do it better than anyone else has before. Believe in your abilities to take an idea and make it greater.

Following these concepts will develop hope for your purpose, but ultimately you need a persistent approach to an extraordinary purpose that is inside you. Again, are you ready to pull your purpose out? Your answer is yes because this is motivational food, food for your soul to birth that purpose that is predetermined on your life. Embrace the opportunities that are presented before you. I do not care about what happened to you in the past. Your time is now and do not blow off the moment. Do you know that if you are at the right place at the right time that can be the beginning of your purpose? Are you late for everything you do? Does success scare you? Can you handle your purpose? It's funny how we ask to be elevated from one step to another, but when given the opportunity, we revert back to that victimized thought process of what all can possibly go wrong. This book is here to present you a thought process of accepting everything that can go right with your purpose.

Let's play a game called follow the leader. I need you to identify a person or persons who are living their passion out in the same or similar area that you aspire. Then I need you to find out what you can learn to enhance your purpose. The successful leaders had to learn how to follow before they became great. Are you humble and hungry enough to follow the leader to live your purpose? The answer is yes again because your purpose will lead you to the top after you follow the leader.

I need you to imagine that your purpose is as essential as an amateur athlete trying to beat a professional on an obstacle course. The professional steps up to the line, next he/she is waiting for the sound of the horn to soar so the obstacle course can begin. However, before he/she can start the obstacle course, things need to be in place. The time keeper needs to get in place, the crowd needs to be strategically planted so they will not impede on his/her time. The obstacles need to be inspected so there are no accidents. The host needs to be ready to make the announcement that the obstacle course is ready to begin. These are all the priorities that need to be in place, this will help the amateur prepare for his/her feat to beat and surpass the professional.

Learn how to get things in order before you attempt to do the impossible. This is an opportunity for the amateur to watch and prepare themselves for greatness. I have listened to countless tapes, listened to 1000's of videos, read many books, and lastly paid to see others speak. The preparation for greatness is oftentimes harder than performing/presenting your gift. These are the intangible things that most spectators never get a chance to see. This brings us to our final (P) **Priorities.**

Priorities plural noun:

1. A thing that is regarded as more important than another.
2. The fact or condition of being regarded or treated as more important.
3. The right to take precedence or to proceed before others.
4. Priority is given to those with press passes and VIPs.

What priorities have you put in place to take your life from one step to the next? I need you to dig deep down inside your mind and determine if you set a strategic plan in motion to make your life better. If you have not then you are wasting time. We cannot hope for the best we have to plan and prioritize to become the best. People often say, "Money can't buy you happiness," and I agree. But I also know, that poverty cannot help you live your passion. Prioritize for greatness. We should make this a bumper sticker slogan. My purpose is to be one of your resources to assist you to taking your life up a notch.

I need to provide you with the 3C's that can assist you with prioritizing. You must **Consider, Control and Connect** because if you follow this blueprint it will align your passion, with your purpose so now you can begin to prioritize.

Consider the possibility of you being successful. It first starts in your mind. You know that image you have inside of you that we sometimes let lie dormant for years. Are you afraid of success because you have considered failing as an option? Well, I am here to tell you that failing is not your battle anymore. Your next move will be intentional because from this day forth, you will consider success by prioritizing. Consider that one feeling that keeps you up at night; you know that feeling of you making it to the top. I need you to start considering that if YOU did everything in order, prioritizing will increase your chances of succeeding up to 75%. Why did I use 75%? I am glad you asked because the 75% is the halfway point between 50 and 100. I am speaking to winners so, therefore; winners will always be greater than. Consider that after today you now have a 75% chance of being great. Do you like those odds? If you said yes then you now have a **Greater Than** 50% chance to be successful. However, it's less than 100%, but let's be realistic. Is anything 100% guaranteed anymore? Living with these odds mixed with prioritizing, I believe that someone else will invest the other 25% into your life. We will talk about investors in your life later in the book. Considering success is one thing but the biggest challenge most people experience is controlling his/her ego during the process. I have an important question to ask you, do you run down a steep heel fast or slow? I hope you said neither because the answer is that you run down a steep hill under **CONTROL**. I know control is hard to do sometimes but it requires practice. I want you to start preparing in the direction in which you want to see your life.

Control your emotions because they will be tested during this stretch. Prioritizing requires action. You and I know that there will be some if not many obstacles you need to hurdle to achieve your mission. Some people always say that the quickest way to get from point A to point B is a straight line. If you're talking mathematically, yes. But in life, you cannot control external factors that happen in your life but you can control your internal factors. Your ability to control your emotions will propel you one step closer to fulfilling your mission. Can you imagine a clock in your head? If so, place your mission on 12:00 o'clock because your mission should stay on your mind day and night. You need a mission you can say good morning and good night too. Isn't it funny how society has allowed different things control over the way some people think or react. You cannot think of an example, I can. There is this device that is designed to make a sound/noise to alert us to react daily if we control it. This device is called an alarm clock. We have mastered the way we control the alarm clock because we set it to a certain time, day, or even month, to sound off. What if we controlled your future the same way? You can set a day and time to control your destiny. (Beep, Beep, Beep, Beep, Beep) The alarm clock in this book just activated. The controls were set and I need you to react. Control your destiny you have the power. Believe in your power. The world needs your power to connect too.

> "Living life under control means you are living with a purpose."
> -Ernest D. Sullivan-

Controlling your ego is the main ingredient to sustain success. How many people do you know of that have experienced some success and lost it all? They generally lost it because of a lack of self-control. It has not escaped any profession. I have seen lawyers become disbarred, doctors sued for malpractice claims, athletes lose contracts and endorsements, and even spiritual leaders who used and abuse people fall and crumble. So what makes another person believe that his/her ego will prevail? Controlling your thoughts, will keep you focused on the Mission because the obstacles that is before you cannot always be predicted. You have to prepare for the unknown and still have a since of control to deal with it. A loss of control happens to a person who only seeks Fame. I am here to tell you that if you keep control of your ego it will increase your chances of fulfilling your mission. Now are you out of control or under control? Ask yourself this question, how can your Mission ever manifest if there is no one for it to **Connect** too?

Connect comes from the word connection, you must have a Mission that connects because if it does not there will never be a connection. Have you ever played the game Connect the Dots? What was the end goal? Was it to miss a dot here or there, or was it to strategically connect one dot to the next. I know it sounds simple but you and I know that everybody was not good at this game. You could have two figures identical and have two people to perform the same task and often some of the figures will not be identical at the end. I have good news, when you connect all of your dots your Mission will be formed to connect with others. You have to connect the dots with the right people. To effectively connect most things, there cannot be any shortcuts. Also, you cannot start to connect the dots for your mission if you bypassed any of the first steps. If you never consider greatness, how can you achieve it? Living what you love is your passion, giving meaning to passion gives it purpose, and aligning it all up requires priorities. Put a plan into place to reach your goal, it will not happen unless you prioritize. Then you should have a visual of how the vision should look and be able to start connecting the dots.

Now, be honest with yourself what (C) are you currently on, is it **Consider, Control** or **Connect**? The 3 C's are only geared toward people who are seeking to fulfill their mission. I am awake from my dream and now I want to Make it Happen. I am so glad that I connected with you because without you I cannot complete my puzzle for success. Are you beginning to see a clearer picture? You are the main power source in your life and taking your life up a notch is up to you.

CHAPTER 3
Do YOU have the POWER?

"Though nobody can go back and make a new beginning.... Anyone can start over and make a new ending."
-Chico Xavier-

The clock just struck twelve and it happened to have struck twelve on an old clock with a bird in it. Do you know what kind of clock that I am referring to? Well, if you do not, it's called a Coo-Coo Clock. Some people will enjoy a Coo-Coo Clock and it will annoy others. People who look for fame are sometimes associated with being called a Coo-Coo Clock because of their timing. The bird that comes out of the Coo-Coo Clock only Coo-Coos for a certain amount of seconds just like fame appears to the masses of the people which it was connected too. However, if you consider there are other clocks that represents you, me, them, they, and others that does not say a word because we are name brand clocks.

The fact that you are breathing means that you are a brand. Your brand is unique and let me be the first to give you your stamp of approval. I need you to scream silently in your head of your reason for existing. Yes, that gift, the one that is hidden inside of you. Some people have talents that are hidden and will not unleash it to the world. Don't you want to share your gift? That is your tool for success. You are about to be filled with power over your gift. What if I gave you an early disclaimer that this power will not come from me, your parents, your spouse, boyfriend/girlfriend, your children or a friend? Your power will come from what is inside you. Are you ready for the **P.O.W.E.R**?

Power is a noun:

1. The ability to do something or act in a particular way, especially as a faculty or quality.
2. The capacity or ability to direct or influence the behavior of others or the course of events.
3. Supply (a device) with mechanical or electrical energy.
4. Move or travel with great speed or force.

Push that positive energy out of you so you can make a difference in this world. Don't just live; you need to live with power. I need you to control your destiny and allow your power to be seen. Do not let your battery go dead when YOU are the power source.

Operate with a divine purpose because your gift is not for you, it's for the world to see. Stop being selfish. Share your gift because what good is it to have a gift without others to share it with you. If the lights never came on how much could you see? (Click) I just saw your light come on. Now reveal yourself.

Withstand the pressure that you may feel while sharing your gift. It's funny but when you are gifted it comes with a certain level of scrutiny. You can do it because you were built for it. That why it is so important to connect with the right people. Remember you cannot control what others do, but you have the power to control what you do.

Eliminate all negative people and forces that have ever told you that you could not do it. It's your gift and they cannot stop it. The only person that can keep a stronghold on you, is you. You are the common denominator as you can tell. You are the boss of you, act like and only hire qualified people to assist you on this journey to the top.

Relating to people is the most important part of your power. Your gift should inspire and make a person(s) feel good after witnessing your gift. If you can give it your best and receive thumbs up, a smile, a card, or even a phone call by one person, than you are connected.

TAKING YOUR LIFE UP A NOTCH
"The Sky Is The Limit For You"

The power is yours but only you can claim it. I can remember a story when I was 31 years old and this homeless man asked me for some money to feed him. My initial reaction was no. I walked passed him without breaking stride. Then all of a sudden I receive an email from the universe to turn around and go and talk to this man. I doubled-back and headed toward him. As I approached him, he put his head down. He gave me the impression that he was thinking, *I already asked him before. He is going to say no again.* I said, "Excuse me sir. Can I talk to you?" He said, "Sure sir."

This was astonishing to me of how polite he was to a person who just minutes ago shrugged him off with a fast, no, without hesitation. I proceeded to sit and we talked for about an hour and, yes, I sat on the ground with him and I found out something amazing. This man was homeless because he sold his house, his car, and his boat to help his two sons that were in legal trouble. I sat there in amazement because I was almost at a loss for words. Then the gift activated I said to the man,

> "Your Sacrifice will bring you the biggest reward you have ever seen."
> -Ernest D. Sullivan-

The man started crying and said, "I receive that sir." I said, "My name is Ernest, sir." I then gave the man money to eat and I walked away with the greatest gift a person can have, and that is **POWER.** That was my very first quote that I took sole custody of, but it remains my best because I did not mention that I gave the man my number and he contacted me years later and I could not recall who he was by his voice. But then he reminded me that, sacrifice will bring you the biggest reward you ever received and I started to get teary-eyed. This man said this is Jerry and do you know that I am now living in Arlington Texas with my two sons and because of what you said gave me the strength to leave this corner and start searching for a new beginning. That was the day that I knew, motivating others is my Passion. I have never shared this story with anyone until now. What day did or will you discover your POWER? I say start right now because your best is yet to come.

I want to dedicate this just for MEN. I hope you will find value with this because a strong man can bring about change. Men it's time to take the POWER back that has been removed from some communities. There are too many young boys who are misguided and lead astray because of not having a strong man around. You are not a man if you allowed the community that you reside in to become victimized because of the people who live in the environment. It's time to change the environment, I have an acronym for the word MEN.

-Make Everything Necessary-

Men should be tired of hearing the "**What if's**." I am going to help us men change the narrative surrounding some communities. I want to provide men with the new **7 "What ifs"** that provides hope for our young men.

- What if all men decided to take care of his sons and daughter?
- What if all men valued education that can inspire his son(s) or daughter(s) to immolate?
- What if all men maintained his role as the provider and protector of his family? This will provide a map for his son(s).
- What if all men believed in family values and passed those traits down to his children?
- What if all men lived their Passion to show his children how happiness starts from enjoying what a person was placed on earth to do?
- What if all men showed respect to themselves and the women in their life. This will set an example for his son(s).
- What if all men showed and expressed their spiritual side so his son(s) could see the **POWER** in faith?

The time has come for men to stop making excuses and make a plan. Do you know of a man that has all the POWER but do not use it? This question should be asked to both men and women because if you activate your Power then you can have **AUTHORITY** over all the myths surrounding the "What if's" that any person may face. This is what separates successful men from unsuccessful men. Do you ever think about taking your life up a notch?

I have just boarded on this 747 aircraft and its destination is to **The Sky is the Limit Boulevard.** It was instructed not to take-off until it has a full plane. Men we cannot leave until successful men are ready. I need your help, my journey cannot continue without you. Have you ever been in a situation where you were ready to go somewhere exciting and you could not leave because you were waiting on others? Did you want to just leave them? I know the answer is yes, but for some reason you stayed. I will tell you why you stayed, it was because anytime you are going on a journey you want someone to take the trip with you.

The Journey, wait, did I mention that every passenger that will be traveling with you needs a boarding pass for this journey. Can I work for you and be the ticket agent handing out the tickets? I want to provide you with a snapshot of the boarding criteria of what items that can be carried on the aircraft. I decided a long time ago that not every person deserve to travel on your journey with you.

- Any person(s) that has hate in their hearts cannot travel. (Haters, naysayers, dream busters, and doubters.)
- Any person(s) that will not support your mission cannot travel. (You have been there for them but the one time you needed them, they abandoned you.)
- Any person(s) that cannot add value on your journey cannot travel. (Your meter needs to be energized.)
- Any person(s) that cannot provide some encouragement during the trials and tribulations cannot travel. (We can motivate ourselves, but sometimes we need someone to talk to is all we ask for.)
- Any person(s) that only wants to travel to see you fail cannot travel. (Believe it or not there are some people around you that just to see you fail.)
- Any person(s) that does not have the drive to continue to learn cannot travel. (People who developed a, I am content spirit are not built for the journey.)

Our journey has to be filled with teammates. I want to be on your team and you are invited to be on my team. Can I issue the boarding passes to the people we want on our journey now?

- **Teammates** that will love you unconditionally. (These are the people that will be with you through our ups and the downs.)

- **Teammates** that will support and challenge you. (You need people around you to make you better.)
- **Teammates** that feed you mentally and spiritually. (You need the balance of knowing that someone is truly concerned about you.)
- **Teammates** that motivate you to continue. (You need people to encourage you not to give up on you.)
- **Teammates** that are there to see you succeed genuinely. (You need to attract people who support your mission.)
- **Teammates** that is willing to take the wheel if you need them too. (Success comes with a price, and you cannot be cut in half. But a better half will do.)

I need you to develop thin patience for anyone not supporting your mission. I encourage a loving spirit, but I do not want you to sacrifice yourself to please someone else. The worst feeling many people experience are regrets. Leave everything on the line when it comes to you and let your gift speak louder than you do.

Your journey begins and ends with who you are issuing out the boarding passes in your life which will help you impact others. I am asking you to look to your heart when deciding how your journey will start and end.

CHAPTER 4
Will YOU follow your Heart?

"You will never follow your inner voice until you clear up the doubts in your mind...."
-Roy T Bennett-

Have you ever been anxious, angry, aggravated or agitated? I hope you understand what needs to be done. Your thoughts of how you envision yourself will become an everlasting image that will remain in your head. I am here to introduce ways to balance how we can allow external factors to live inside of us. It all starts by taking the first step. The first step is sometimes the hardest but after you get your momentum going it gets easier. I want to give you **8 small steps** to Take Your Life Up a Notch!

> Step 1: Believe in yourself;
> Step 2: Invest in your gift;
> Step 3: Create a support system;
> Step 4: Focus on results;
> Step 5: Ask for help;
> Step 6: Set achievable goals;
> Step 7: Take your first step; and
> Step 8: Follow your heart.

> "It isn't the mountains ahead to climb that wear you out; it's the pebble in your shoe."
> -Muhammad Ali-

Believing in yourself is the only way that you can get from one point to another in your life. This is not the time for you to continue with what happened in the past. Let's concentrate on believing and achieving now. Your car has been parked in neutral for far too long. Many other features drive you. Your beliefs, ambition, and your drive are all you need. You are at the starting point of your growth stage. You have hoped, wished, desired, anticipated, and sought after all in your mind. But I need you to conform to the feeling that has handcuffed you, BELIEFS. I believe in you because your gift is not yours, it's for me and the rest of the world to see. Do not rob us by keeping your gift to yourself.

What if I told you that I believe in you? I do. I am asking you to believe how powerful a pencil can be compared to a pen or marker. Believe me. I am glad to be a pencil with all the attachments. On this journey called life you will have moments that you will want to forget whatever happened. The new you have just received the add-on eraser.

I know a prominent artist and he said that even if he makes a mistake, he can still make his picture turn out good. He said he believes he has the ability to shade in the mistake and oftentimes his piece comes out looking better. I am here to tell you to believe in yourself because any past mistakes can be shaded in because you are reading this. Use your eraser/beliefs and start on your journey. I want you to be able to inspire others by saying because of you, they chose not to quit. Your ability to keep pushing forward will help someone else.

Investing in your gift is the best way to take your dream out of your head and turn it into a reality. It may take some longer than others to do this but if you are down to your last dime, with nowhere to go, no purpose driving your life, why not insert your next deposit into yourself. How much more can you withstand? Are you ready for this journey? Ask me how much will it cost you, and I will give you the answer. It costs **TIME**. Start by investing your time to see what avenues you need to take to begin your journey. I want to provide you with ways you can invest in yourself.

- Go back to school;
- Get a mentor;
- Do some volunteer work;
- Accept an internship;
- Read and Relate; and
- Start your vision board.

Those 6 ways to invest in your gift are game changers. Yes, I left money off the list for a reason. Your gift will make room for you. You will be surprised at how much money will start falling in your lap. If you do the following and understand that the same prefix that is in IN-Vest is IN-YOU, then you just received your boarding pass. By following your dream, the money will come. It may sound like it will take a long time, but trust me your life can turn around in a blink of an eye. Just remember that for every no you receive, you will be that much closer to your, yes. I need you to find people with the same mental disorder as you, SUCCESS.

> "Stop walking around being insufficient when you have a sufficient gift inside of you."
> -Ernest D. Sullivan-

Creating a support system can make the difference between success and failure. Have you ever heard that association brings on assimilation? This was true 100 years ago and it stands true today. Surround yourself around people who can help you, not hurt you. Your circle should consist of a wide-range of Teammate's. These Teammates must all possess a purpose on the Journey to Taking your life up a Notch Boulevard. Who was the last person to call you and offer to help you without you calling them first? I can only imagine how your face looks right now. Your team has to have a few components to be effective for you.

Component 1: A genuine interest in your success **(Mentor)**.

Component 2: A resourceful person that can lead you to the source (**Manager**).

Component 3: A loving person that you can share your ideas with (**Motivator**).

You are the CEO of your life. Now, all you need is your board of directors in place to see that YOU keep your eyes on the prize, The Mission. The runway to success is right in front of you. Are you ready?

Your **Mentor's** sole purpose should be to hold you accountable of what YOU say you want to do with your life. He/she should set aside an appointed day and time to meet with you monthly to discuss progress. An extra note is, these meetings should continue after you reach your initial goal. The hardest part will not be reaching your destination, it will be staying the course and excelling.

Your **Manager's** purpose is to help you manage your activities because you are smart, but even you need some help. This is the person that is not afraid to tell you that you are right/wrong. Some people have the common thinking error that their way is always the best way. You should reverse your thoughts to allow a certain person(s) in authority to assist you.

Your **Motivator's** purpose is to encourage you on those bad days that are sure to come. Life is complicated but can be managed. Ask yourself, have you ever seen a storm that did not pass over? Me either. Your motivator will just reaffirm you that things will work out. Do me a favor and trust them. I do.

Focusing on results will not only allow you to stop worrying because if you know that your Life is being taken up a notch then the Sky is the Limit for you. I always use the reality of 6 plus 3, 5 plus 4, and 8 plus 1 as a road map for my life. I do not care how you add them up, they all will equal up to 9. I encourage you to develop a mindset to stop worrying about things that you or I have no control over. The one thing we do have control over is the end results.

I can remember a time when I was in college and it use to amaze me on how every person learned differently. I am the kind of learner who needs to see it done, but I learned that others could hear it being done and we both came out with a similar conclusion. The conclusion in this scenario was our grade. That alone got me to realize that just because a person does it this way, does not mean that they are doing it wrong. Here are some ways to approach your life when dealing with end results.

- First, set short-term and long-term goals;
- Second, give yourself a realistic time frame to achieve that goal;
- Third, learn how to accept adversity and use it as fuel to get to the goal;

- Forth, revisit your end goal quarterly to keep you on track with your purpose; and
- Fifth, do not be afraid to start over.

I understood that in life we can use our imagination because if we are traveling by train from Chicago, Illinois to Hollywood, California the train will oftentimes have to make stops along the way to refill, change conductors, pick up additional passengers, might experience some unexpected mechanical problems etc.... Your life is similar; you may have to switch tracks from where you originally started to refocus to something else that has similar value. You may have to drop some people out of your life and you may have to pick others up along the way on your journey. You may experience a few setbacks because of an illness, financial instabilities, and you may even have to change directions. But at the end, if you make it to the destination, you have accomplished your mission.

Are you afraid of asking for help? If you are not afraid always revisit the five (5) ways to approach life when dealing with adversity.

Asking for help will sometimes save your life. Do you know that so many people allow their ego's to dictate their reactions to both their successes and failures? If you don't know something, ask. Asking allows others to look at you as being a viable leader. Not asking allows others to look at you as being arrogant. The moment you say, *can't nobody tell me anything*, is the moment you have lost your ability to grow. I need to ask you a question. When was the last time you asked for help? I want to provide all of you who do not know what to ask for with 10 things to ask for on the **ASK LIST.**

- Ask for forgiveness;
- Ask for peace;
- Ask for resources;
- Ask for directions;
- Ask for sponsorships;
- Ask for a positive relationship;
- Ask for a career and not a job;
- Ask to be taken higher up in your life;
- Ask for all that's owed to you to be given; and
- Ask for change.

Do not feel ashamed because I ask for all these things in my life. We can ask together. Your next goal that you set, make it an achievable goal. I listened to Steve Harvey on a Facebook video and he spoke about bags of stuff a person never received because they did not ask for it. The next opportunity you get to ask someone that can help you for help, ask. All he/she can say is, yes or no. How do I know they will say, yes, ask to find out? Hint

Setting achievable goals is not only a saying; it's the way to go from one level to the next. This is the captain speaking and welcome on your journey to **The Sky is the Limit Boulevard.** As we are traveling we may experience some turbulence, and I want to prepare you for the actions that may need to be taken. While flying if we are traveling at 30,000 feet altitude and if the turbulence arises, we may have to gradually ELEVATE up to 40,000 feet of altitude. The captain gave instructions because of the potential problems that may arise. The just in case instructions, because they know if he/she did not explain it and it happened then the passengers would go into a frenzy. But did you catch the key word, *Gradually.* If he elevates too fast the cabin pressure may be too much and the passengers may pass out. Sometimes we have to accept success gradually because if given to fast you will not know how to handle certain situations. Allow yourself time to grow and perfect your gift.

Your journey is no different, I am imagining my phone ringing and it's YOU on the line and you expressed to me that you are lost. My first question would be to you, where are you. Because if you cannot tell me where you are, then how can I help you? Set goals whereas they can be reached and someone can help you reach them if you ask. It all starts with the one person that matters, YOU! Your next step should be intentional. Are you ready for the climb?

Taking your first step will oftentimes be the hardest, but understand if you do not, you will remain in the same place. So now I need you to put your back foot in motion so I can push you. Because if you are not in motion and I push you, you might fall on your face. Have you ever felt like you fell on your face? Me too, I have failed so much that I have to keep my life moving so I will not fall again. Did you notice I use both *fell* and *failed* in one sentence after the other?

"Failing is a part of life, but falling on purpose is a choice."
-Ernest D. Sullivan-

Are you ready to go? Remember as kids you had to countdown to begin the race. You are now at the starting blocks and you have warmed up, are you ready? Your race cannot start until YOU are ready. When was the last time you witnessed a baby take his or her first steps. Tell the truth, you were more excited than the baby. I am excited for you because I know that you just received your boarding pass. Can I be a passenger on your journey? I am asking for it. Your first steps are important because you want someone around to witness them. What good to have a life changing moment and no one got to see where it all began? Take your smart phone out and record your first step. The picture should show a still picture with you looking in the direction in which you are going, UP. I am here to tell you that **The Sky is the Limit for You!**

This gives me something to look forward too. I want to follow you, but I need you to follow your heart.

Following your heart is probably one of the hardest/easiest things to do. I know because we have what's called responsibilities that sometimes hold us back. There has to come a time that is strategically planned out when responsibilities are the drivers. Please understand the one thing about life is, it will change, however, your best is yet to come. Place your heart on warm because when anything gets hot, something happens. Have you had a fuzzy feeling but you did not know why, it was your strongest muscle, your heart. Believe what is in your heart because it has turned ideas into reality, it has changed boyfriends/girlfriends into spouses, it has changed a poor person into a rich person, and it can take your Life up a Notch if you just follow it. The desire you have for success might have you wondering if you made the right decision to follow your heart. I am here to tell you if you do not, you might just wonder forever about following your heart. At this point on your journey things should be getting hot around you. When your heart consults with your brain, it's time for you to move because it's your destiny. So after taking these 8 small steps are you ready to go to the next level?

Are you ready to walk, jog or run because as you start on this mission, you will need a few things to take with you? Can we call your journey a 007 **MISSION**?

CHAPTER 5
Are you ready for your MISSION?

"If you're walking down the right path and you're willing to keep walking, eventually you'll make progress."
-Barack Obama-

The time of hoping is gone; it's time to start your engine. Your appetite has just picked up for success because you are about to receive the meal fit for a King or Queen. Your mission is yours and do not get upset and angry with people who do not support your mission. You need to only socialize with winners because winners accomplish results. I want you to make a wish because with hard work and dedication it will come true. Better yet I would like you to stack the odds higher in your favor that you cannot do anything but be successful. I know what thoughts you had before because I had them too. When we have tried something and it did not work, we tend to not want to try it again. The mistakes I have made as a person has propelled me into the person I am today. Mistakes happen for a reason because without mistakes, there would be no use for correction. Just think the more mistakes you made can be a positive if you learn from them. Making the choice to overcome trials separates success from failure. Your next accomplishments will be far greater than any failures you have experienced by understanding, W.I.S.H.

What
If
Something
Happens!

Have you ever thought about what if something happens this time in your life? I have thought long and hard, and I believe that your time is now. Tie up your shoes, start to stretch, step up to the starting blocks because your Mission starts now. I want you to understand W.I.S.H's as being a permanent fixture of furniture placed in your mind. Stop letting empty thoughts take up space in your brain. Your brain is strong and is the driving force behind your thought process. This is the time to trust your brain because you must think it before it can become reality. You have a couple of options to start your Mission.

Option One- You can start by writing your dreams down and create your vision board. This vision should give directions on how you will start and end your mission. I suggest again that you start with believing in yourself because if you do not believe in yourself it will become difficult for someone else to believe in your mission. Your beliefs are the final frontier of your thoughts. Hoping can only get you so far, it's time to start believing it will happen. I remember waking up one day saying these words, "I don't have nothing to do today." I then started thinking if I have not made it from point A to point B traveling towards my mission, then Yes I do have something to do today. Do you have something to do today? Your mission requires a daily dose of commitment. The moment you take your thoughts off your mission will be the day that you have to restart your engine. The engine is design to perform better once it gets going. Have you ever noticed that when the winter time comes and you decide to turn the heat on for the first time of the season, it takes a while before it heats up the house? It's not because it's broken, it's because the heat has been lying dormant over the summer months. This could be your dreams lying dormant waiting to be turned on. This should make you believe that if you just turn on your mission it may drive itself to success if you are available to start it into motion.

"The worst thoughts in this world are to live in a world with regrets."
-Ernest D. Sullivan-

Option Two- Developing a care about what others said about you to discourage you from beginning your mission is just them being a dream-destroyer. The dreams that are destroyed are not from the cause of someone else, it's because of you. I am asking you to take full responsibilities for what happens in your life. I did not say remember the past either, your thoughts right now will either make your life better or destroy your mission. I do not want you to abort your mission because of someone else. You are the CEO of your life. I feel it getting warmer because you have now taken control and the Mission is on. I need you to make sure your Mission is of relevance because if your mission is to be manifested, it better be for the good of this world. Yes, I promote positive outcomes for all people that will gain from your mission. Why buy a new car, then drive it off the lot and then jump out of it while it's rolling. Yes, a person was excited about their new car, but when they jumped out and left it role, they never looked to see where it was going to stop. You do not want your mission to be something that hurt others. Your mission should be filled with a Mission Statement of love. Seek to add value because your mission is a direct reflection of you.

I just received another email from the universe and it reads, smile because the mission is on for many motivated people and you and I can witness it. I see doctors, lawyers, writers, designers, athletes, teachers, mentors, CEO's, speakers, computer techs, engineers, nurses, psychologists, enlisted service people, entrepreneurs, screenwriters, and most of all great people. Your mission is a light for so many others, so I declare that you release it to the world because what good is a treasure buried if nobody ever finds it. I am a hunter and I have the ability to find almost anything, and I think you have something that I am looking for. Remember, you are the most important person in your life.

The pre-celebration has begun because you have just started your engine. Are you thinking about your party? The party will have a variety of things that is going on for entertainment. You now will have to decide what entertainment would not only satisfy your laughter, but your guests as well. I have attended a few in my life and I have noticed that sometimes allowing unwanted guest to attend your celebration is the recipe for disaster. You will be amazed at the people who clap for you, sing for you and even praise you to your face, but behind your back, despise you. Please have your guest to RSVP because you then can dictate who you want at the celebration. Your mind works so use it correctly because a misguided mind is like a shoe without laces. Keep your mind sharp because if its loose like shoe laces then it will allow things to get into it and most importantly you may lose some things you were trying to keep secret. Think about it, we sometimes had to hide our money or the key to our house in our shoe.

Your Mission will require something else which is a positive tongue. The things that you say out of your mouth can change the outcome of your mission. I need you to develop a vocabulary of words that expresses belief because the moment you allow the negative thoughts to flow they will hinder your mission. I would like to give you several (I's) that should be a part of you traveling towards your mission.

- I will be successful;
- I am ready;
- I can do anything;
- I did it;
- I know my mission;
- I will make a difference;
- I can help others;
- I will give it my best shot daily;
- I made mistakes, and it paid off, I learned; and
- I am glad I chose not to quit.

The thought of knowing you will be successful is a base hit in the game of baseball on your way to fulfilling your mission. Many people have stepped up to the plate, but allowed a strike out to stop them from stepping back up to the plate. When you step up this time be ready because you saw most of the pitches/obstacles before. I know sometimes things will be thrown at you that you were not ready for, but if you are ready for the mission then you will find a way to make contact. This is why believing is so important because you can do anything that you put your mind to do.

TAKING YOUR LIFE UP A NOTCH
"The Sky Is The Limit For You"

Now, let's switch sports because sometimes basketball is played faster than baseball. I declare that you claim what you can do because for some this is your best opportunity to make the shot. I am here to give you the assistance that you need to make the shot. Are you ready to shoot? Now I need you to check your mailbox for your returns of all the guests you sent your RSVP's out too. Hitting the shot is one thing but hitting a shot without anybody to witness it has a meaning too. It simply could mean that a person got so caught up in the Fame that they forgot about their Mission. I would like to be around to see you hit the shot. Then I need you to do me a favor and let me tell the world that YOU DID IT. People who make things happen almost never have to bring up what he or she accomplished because the guest that RSVP'd will do it for them. That's when you can stay true to the cause and only say that "YOU" were only focused on the Mission. Always aim to help others because you only are as good to those you help along the way. Do not make the same mistake more than once. I only want to hear you say (I) when you are telling someone that you chose not to quit. Since I know you will not quit, now you are ready to board the plane?

CHAPTER 6
Have you decided to Take Your Life up a Notch?

"The biggest adventure you can take is to live the life of your dreams."
-Oprah Winfrey-

You are not the same person you were five years ago, last year, last month, last week, or even yesterday you have grown a little stronger every day. How strong are you today? I know you are stronger because you woke up to see another day. Your strength will never be measured by your physical strength; it's oftentimes measured by what is inside of you. Can you remember a time that you did something or got through something tough and you just did not know how you did it? I can tell you how you did it, it's called **Growing**. Now ask yourself, how much have you grown and how much more do you want to grow? You should be reinventing yourself after each accomplishment. Do you know that hard work and perseverance allows our mind to grow? I know that you are on your way to taking your life up a notch and, therefore, you still have a lot of growing to do. I said it before, and I will say it again, I have never seen a dog chase a parked car. You are a motivator, a leader, a coach, a world-changer, a gift to this world. I need you to keep growing. I would like to give you 6 ways that you can tell if you have grown.

1. **If you are no longer afraid of failing/failure**, then you have grown. Oftentimes we can be delivered from something or someone and still allow the ghost of the past to dictate our future. You cannot go another day worrying about passing/failing, winning/losing, success/failure, and happiness/comfortability because the moment this exist, you are still afraid to grow. Now if you are no longer afraid of passing, winning, success, and happiness then you are not afraid to take your life up a notch. You are stronger than you think or look but knowing how strong you are will eliminate the doubt that sometimes tries to seep through the back of your head. Ask yourself what was the last thing that you were or still are afraid of? I now challenge you today, tomorrow, and the next day to confront it now. Note, I did not say if you are no longer afraid of a person because your life cannot be elevated to the next level with another human being if you are afraid of people. Your

elevation will start when you start looking in the direction in which your passion lies.

2. **If you accept the fact that you are chosen**, then you have grown. I just read a story about a man that was homeless for ten years and now he owns three restaurants. Can you say chosen. Sometimes it may require a little more growth for some of you before you can take your life up a notch. Do you know that some things are easier to put together than others, and your mission can be like putting together an entertainment system? You are your own entertainment system. You know when the entertainment systems are on display at the store, they look good, but when you get it home, and it's in a box, they are hard to put together. The moment you stop being afraid, you just open the new entertainment *System/You*, but if you know people like I do, there will always be that one person that wants to remove steps in the building process. When you are chosen, you have to be careful who you choose to help put your mission together. Because if they do not put you together tight enough, you will eventually fall apart. Your strength is

not in question, but on your way to taking your life up a notch, you cannot get there without the help of others. However, if you choose the right person(s) to help *YOU*, then they will be chose amongst a chosen few that will remain important.

3. **If you are not envious or jealous of others,** then you have grown. You cannot covet over someone else's success. This is really a task for some people who want to be leaders because they want it because it looks good on someone else. The envious thoughts that Mike thinks he is something because he has a car, a truck, and bucks but that do not give the next person the right to have it. Who do Michelle think she is because she has this, that, and a hat? In fact it should not give you or me the idea that the things they have would look better on either of us. This type of attitude will send a person back to *Ground-Zero*. I do not want to lose my place in the order of success because I am envious of someone else. Believe it, your track to success can and will get blocked if you consume your life worrying about another person. You will get that later. You need to always keep your eyes on the prize because

their success is an image; your success will become your reality. It all goes back to being chosen. The things that other people have, say, or do have absolutely nothing to do with you or me on their journey. Your journey to taking your life up a notch cannot begin until a person eliminates jealousness and envy from their life. The growth occurs when you can embrace, encourage, and examine how they did or got it and genuinely mean it. Then you have grown.

4. **If you accept opportunities over people**, then you have grown. This may be the easiest way to see growth in your life. The moment you stop worrying about what people say then you have grown. As painful as this may sound, it may be someone you love. Ideally, you want them on your team as part of your board of directors/family/friends to support your mission. News flash, sometimes your board cannot handle your growth. The opportunities are in front of you, but apprehension from others can sometimes delay your strength. I have come across many strong people, but are weaken by their board of directors. Remember, you are the CEO of your mission. They are oftentimes

the ones you are doing it for. So you prepare yourself for the opportunity to change lives because the strength is inside you. The next time any person ask you what do you do for a living, say this in response, "Whatever it takes." Your next opportunity is closer than you think. From this day forward remove your dark glasses and prepare your vision to receive provision. You must be ready for the opportunity that is coming your way.

5. **If you are able to forgive others** and move on, then you have grown. No one is perfect and I will be the first to say that I had challenges with forgiving people I felt wronged me. I have strength to forgive but the heartaches to remember. This is a touchy subject and many strong people never want to admit they are weak in this area. Forgiving is part of the process to grow and to exceed all expectations you have on your journey. Sometimes it's that one hurdle/task that you cannot get over because you have something, or someone holding you down. The growth has been shown through many aspects of your life, but this unforgiving bug will eat you up from the inside. Let it go and grow, or keep

it in and keep saying when. The when is now for you, ask yourself, are you ready to take your life up a notch? You can no longer allow your frustrations in others to prohibit you from moving forward. Look at forgiving as if it was a hard exam you failed and had to retake. When you pass the exam, you pass the test. You are now relieved that you finished a chapter in your life that you can move on from. Is your heart clear and free? Whenever you say or said you forgive you have grown.

6. **If you understand the meaning of sacrifice**, then you have grown. You may have to give up on a few people, places, and things because remember the vision is yours. Can you remember a time when you had to be somewhere important and you told someone and they said something as simple as that's great? They probably meant it, but did they really care about how you were getting there versus the reward from what you will get when you got there. Some people will not ask the initial question of how because it's your destiny. You must understand that you are the purpose and the prize. Are you ready to be unwrapped so the world can see the gift inside?

You sometimes have to make it a surprise because oftentimes when the prize is revealed too soon it loses value. On your journey to taking your life up a notch you should market yourself as a Mercedes Benz or a Bentley car because they almost never advertise their worth to the public. I have learned that while sacrificing you need to concentrate on these few things; meditating, fasting, and communicating with your mission. This is the perfect way to build strength. Remember the goal is to grow stronger. You cannot rely on the success of someone else to make you great. When was the last time you made a sacrifice? What was the sacrifice? Did you achieve your desired outcome? Yes, questioning your sacrifices give a clearer indication of how strong you are. Can you be convinced to make one more sacrifice? Now that you have arrived at the airport and have your boarding pass, your sacrifice is to reach your destination stronger and prepared. You heard it here first; the sky is the limit for you because you decided to sacrifice.

Have anyone ever assumed who you are before asking you what you stand for. It happens quite frequently because sometimes past behaviors are indicators for others to judge you eternally. While taking your life up a notch you have a decision to make. Do you want to have your story told by others, or do you want to take the wheel and drive your own story? Did you know that life is a story? Now is the time to define your story the way you want it to end. Sometimes our story will have different twists and plots that are amusing and other times we can have action scenes, but the one plot you should avoid is the drama scenes. You will become hindered if you are entertaining drama in your story. Drama cannot occur with you alone, it requires other **characters.** I wanted to introduce the word characters because these are the cast of professionals, amateurs, and extras that are needed to have a successful story.

Most people will not be honest and tell their story, but I will share a little of my story. Do not get excited, this story will not be a tell-all affair whereas you can start judging me. From childhood to manhood I would always dream about successful ventures in my life, I envisioned being great. I always had a presence around family and friends but sometimes I was not presented with relevance. I was the type of leading character as a child and still to this day that could play the role of a leader if I choose too. I oftentimes felt like the other characters in my story would not like me if I took the leading role. It's funny how your passion will drive you in the direction of your destiny. The moment I accepted my leading role, I gained knowledge. I had finally embraced my purpose for living because for many years I settled for a lesser role. Do not act in another scene of your life wondering or accepting any role. Your new role has to compliment your strengths because your gifts and talents are now exposed.

Ask yourself, at any point in your life, have you dreamed of completing an over-the-wall hurdle during an obstacle course? For many years, I have had that same dream and I could not climb over that wall. I want you to imagine me falling from that wall back down to where I started over, and over, and over again. Did I mention that before I fell back down on the side, I started from a couple of times prior to that I was leading the race during that obstacle course? I must also mention that I had a few chances to get over but chose not to because I did not want to leave behind the cast in my story. I decided then to become a leader. I accepted the fact that I was chosen, I was never jealous or envious of others, I learned how to accept opportunities, I am able to forgive people who wronged me, and I now believe in the power of sacrifice because this is how I chose to take my life up a notch. I want to provide others with the bounce/lift to hurdle any obstacle that is in their way. Your mission also needs to happen. Remove the doubt now; you are the man/woman for the job. Do you believe it, I repeat, do you believe it? I know what happened in the past did not work, but remember W.I.S.H, (What if something happens) this time.

I want to ask you a serious question, how did your story start? I want to provide you with a role in my story by telling yours in this book.

My story started when I decided to take my life up a notch is when

_____
_____
_____
_____
_____
_____
_____
_____
_____
_____
_____
_____
_____
_____
_____
_____
_____
_____
_____
_____
_____
_____
_____

TAKING YOUR LIFE UP A NOTCH
"The Sky Is The Limit For You"

_____
_____
_____
_____
_____
_____
_____
_____
_____
_____
_____.

Let me be the first to say thank you. You just made an important step to continuing your journey of taking your life up a notch. If you would like to share your story with me personally, email me at:
<u>ernestsullivan3@gmail.com</u>

I know you are ready to take off on this journey. Did I mention that there may be some hidden fees before takeoff?

CHAPTER 7
What Price are You willing to Pay?

"There is no magic to achievement. It's about hard work, choices, and persistence."
-Michelle Obama-

The cost of success is not a lot if you are doing it to accomplish your mission. I expressed earlier on how if you put in 75% of your own capital then you can get others to sponsor the remaining 25%. This rings true for any successful large corporation or small business. Even entrepreneurs have found a way to get others to invest in them, (Sponsorships). Yes, I said sponsorships and fundraisers. Here is how different entities secure financial support. (Corporations) They oftentimes allow others to buy shares and stock into their ideas. Start thinking of yourself as a corporation your mission serves the same purpose. (Small Businesses) Others sometimes take on partners to fulfill their missions. Have you ever considered how strong you really are? I want you take a chair with four legs attached and attempt to pick it up by grabbing only one leg from the bottom. I hope your power hand is not shaking. Now, imagine having some partners grabbing the remaining three legs. Your load just got lighter. Allow help when allowing your money to work for you. You can thank me later. Well, I want you to welcome yourself to an upgraded seat in first class on this flight. You now have to decide who you want to help fund your mission. You should know at this point where you are headed so now putting the plan in place is your next phase. The planning stage requires you to have made that initial sacrifice. I want to introduce a **5 Phase Method** to assist you with the cost of taking your life up a notch.

- **Phase 1-** Get a job to help fund your mission. I promote working to obtain some working capital because oftentimes the smallest amount of resources if you do not have it can halt your progress. You need to be able to have a leg to stand on before most people will take you seriously. Have you ever been in a position and you didn't have any money and you called a family member or a friend and they said I can give you some money, but you had to come and get it. Do you see my point you need something but someone offered to help but you do not have gas in your car or money to ride public transportation to go get it. From experience, most often if people that are willing to help you would have apprehension especially if they have to bring it to you they might be bewildered inside. So in this first phase learn how to be ready to receive your reward by being prepared for your destiny. Remember this, your destiny will never be tied to any person who left you because your steps are yours and only you can take that first step.

- **Phase 2-** Learn how to save some money because it often seems like givers with the least are the ones that settles for less. You have to learn how to truly invest in yourself. There is a process to get to your goal. Stop worrying about your situation and concentrate on your destiny. The price to pay is not called investing in your situation it is sacrifice for your passion. I have learned that people are more apt to help you when they see the dedication and sacrifice you have for your trip to the Sky is the Limit Boulevard. That is letting yourself know and your support system know that you are keeping your eyes on the mission. The finish line is near. Do not let obstacles stop you. Taking your life up a notch is not a cliché, it's your mission. Develop a strategy to save because for many people, saving is not an easy thing to do. I have a solution for the people who have a problem with saving. As soon as you get your next pay check from the job you have to fund your mission, go to the bank and ask to open up a new Checking Account and a Certificate Deposit Account

(CD). I did not say savings account because most people have the checking and savings account joined on the same account. The CD comes with a maturity date. You can get a three month to five year CD that has a higher yield than any checking or savings accounts. Earlier, I mention give yourself at least three to six months to get prepared for your journey. This will not be enough to fund your mission, but if you invest at least 25% of your earnings into yourself for the duration then you will have what I call **ACTION MONEY**. Action money is money that can get the movement for investors, partners, or sponsors to consider your brand.

- **Phase 3-** Do not steal from yourself because the price you will pay from stealing from yourself will be far greater than the price for investing in your success. I mentioned Action-Money and if you steal from yourself it becomes money-without-action. Well a person can spend it on something that they want; therefore, it is now money-without-action. Do you know action-money is only used for needs? Let that penetrate overnight and ring it out in the morning. Your drive for success is like a car, a car need to drive forward. Cars cannot want to be driven they need a person to drive it, and so do you. Become a needy person when it comes to saving your money. So, if someone asked for your action-money, tell them I need this money. This money is a game-decider. Save and have a chance at winning or spend it and never make it into the game. I am the author that wrote **Life is About Choices**! The choices people make today does not only affect them today but for some, the rest of their lives.

- **Phase 4-** Teach yourself how to stay calm. Believe it or not your dream can go from a thought on a piece of paper into a reality and even into millions overnight. This will require a certain level of calmness. You have to act like you belong because if you do not people will not take you seriously. The last thing you want to do is invest in yourself and blow-it because you do not have confidence in your abilities to belong. I am not asking you to change for the worse, but a new level brings along a different environment. The sense of calmness is not an easy task to master because you are dealing with your emotions. Have you ever witnessed a baby crying and you could not understand what was wrong? You tried to feed the baby, change the baby, hold the baby, and even rock the baby. However, the baby continued to cry. We will never know but one thing I have witnessed as a father of three is that the baby will continue to cry until they calm down. Perhaps that is what happens to some people, they began to stay up all night worrying about things they have no control over. They began to cry out to any and everybody who will listen to their story. They solicit sympathy via social media (Facebook) for reassurance or pity. Then they become upset when people challenge their thought process because it did not align with their issues. That's why I encourage you to learn to stay calm. You have been given the power to weather any and all storms that comes your way. I know it seems like it's too much, but you have been designed with a fabric that is unique to only you, tough. Learning how to stay calm will allow you to see ahead of you on your destination because fog, rain, turbulence, family, friends, enemies all can play a part in blinding your view. But if you are calm, you can put the windshield wipers on and see your destination.

- **Phase 5-** Learn how to say Goodbye because sometimes we allow people to stay longer than they should on our journeys. This is a lost art because the world has raised uncaring people. Have you ever been taken for granted over and over by someone you thought loved you. The goodbyes are never intended for people you do not love, they are for the people that you confided certain things in and they betrayed you. Those people that whenever they needed you, you were there, but the second you needed them they had an excuse. Sometimes you have to practice saying goodbye because then it can have several meanings. You can say goodbye to family and add, see you later with intentions of seeing them later. I need you to adapt the new goodbye, the goodbye when you express it with these meanings:

- o Goodbye and I want to thank you for leaving my life for good.
- o Goodbye because you have taken me for granted for the last time.
- o Goodbye, I did not know how to before, but I know now that I do not need you.
- o Goodbye and good riddance because you are holding me back.
- o Goodbye and I will make it without you.

I know those goodbye's sounds harsh to say to someone you love or loved, but listen, you do not say this to their face. You proceed on your journey without them. When they begin to see you getting further and further out of their eyesight, trust me they will then say goodbye for you. Have you ever watched a plane take off for the first time? For me it was a fascinating experience because after liftoff, I could see it in the air seeming like it would be in sight forever, but after a while it was gone. You are on your way to taking your life up a notch and you have just lifted off. You following your dreams are the new Goodbye because after you have ascended out of view the people who held you back cannot see where you're headed now. There are no circumstances that cannot be conquered. Think about your last jam you were in, did you make it out? The same way you left that jam behind you, learn to leave people behind and say goodbye. However, make sure you are saying goodbye to the right people.

Sometimes leaving behind people that you love is a hard price to pay for success, but ask yourself this question, will they hold up their dreams for you. For some the answer may have been, yes, but for you the answer could have been, no. You have to make a serious commitment because you can never put a price tag on a mission. You have stayed long enough in the same situation. Why not pay yourself to better your life. You are working a job or have worked a job to better some else's life. Think about it, why continue to get upset about something you can change. I am loaning you your first installment with motivation, and guess what it cost me energy, but it can give you strength. Do you know having the strength to start your journey to taking your life up a notch is worth a lot? But ask yourself one more time, what price are you willing to pay to change your life? You have to be honest because if you know where you are headed you can get help getting to that destination. If you do not know how to get started, I will show you what you need to do while getting ready for your victory. You need to do a self-assessment on yourself and the inventory of what you already have versus what you will need to finance your mission. The things you need are closer than you think. I expressed that it's at least 25% of action – money waiting on you. Ask for it. With this **action-money** available it can take you higher. Some people always think that the people that supposed to help you will, it might be just that person that values your gift. This is that person that believes in you and will sacrifice because of the importance of investing in others. However, you must have a plan. In your plan, it must include the price that you are willing to pay. Now, I need to know where you are headed.

CHAPTER 8
Do You Know Where you are headed?

"It matters not what someone is born, but what they grow to be."
-J.K Rowling-

When you think about your life, what are you thinking? Do you understand that life is worth living if you know where you are going? This chapter explores three elements of why your life is worth living if you know where you are going. There will be a turning point in your life that will give you the choice to make a decision concerning your life and the people you are taking with you.

What is the one thing that you are good at doing? Have you recognized that the destiny is yours and you can leave your mark on this world? You need to fulfill your destiny because you were placed on earth for a reason? You must know that life is worth living because you have uniqueness deep down inside of you that you can pull from to reach the top. You have been awakened from your dream and it's now time to make it happen. From this day forth, you must wake up determine and do not sleep longer than your body requires. I am glad you have arrived to your gate on time traveling on your one-way ticket to The Sky is the Limit Boulevard as your destination. Now that you have learned about your mission and your journeys throughout this book, it's time to Take Your Life up a Notch. You will also need and understand the 3 Elements to get you there.

Element 1

Preparing yourself for what has not happened yet in your life is the first thing you must do. The definition is your guide: To make ready beforehand for a specific purpose, as for an event or occasion. I will play the role of the airline pilot in this chapter to prepare you for takeoff. Attention YOU, and yes, I am talking to you. You are the first passenger to board and I am the pilot for you on your journey to the top. The first thing I hope the gatekeeper took from you was your traveling itinerary because it needs to match the destination that you are traveling. It is really ashamed that some people will have an idea, a vision, a mission, a desire, a fate, and miss the opportunity because he or she is not **Prepared.** A prepared person at a specific time will have a far better chance of reaching their destination. You were provided with a row and a seat assignment on your ticket to success on this flight. Do not get upset if you do not know the passenger who will be sitting beside you in first class. Sometimes when people start his or her journey they want to arrive at the destination faster than anticipated. Remain calm remember because you have to prepare for the person(s) ahead of you before you can move into your success. Preparation requires patience.

I can remember doing everything right as an instructor at a college and things still went imperfectly. I worked for a college that appreciated my demeanor and attitude, but they did not respect my preparation. I was promoted as the Lead Instructor of the business program and from their things went wrong. The person I was promoted over was more qualified and experienced in that role. However, she was the person that insisted that I prepare myself for a different role, not knowing it would be hers. Do you know that sometimes you can prepare for the direction that you are going, but because of someone else's imperfections they may delay your trip? Here is how you solve that problem/issue, you understand that setbacks will and are going to happen in your life. However, the good news is when you finally make it to your destination you will appreciate it more. Then you can reflect back on all the people who made the trip with you or who were let off along the way. You do know that you will have some along the way family, friends, enemies, that were just with you for what could satisfy them. That's why you have to own this element and park this inside of your brain so that you can remain under control. You hidden away some things and that became your protection from future hurt, pain, and anguish that you cannot control. When was the last time you practice on how you would act when you arrive to your destination? Trust me practice.

Element 2

Practicing on how to be great is not a cliché it's an element that you cannot avoid. Most professionals have never become great without practicing and honing their craft. Can you remember as a kid imitating your victory speech when you were rewarded the highest honor from your dream? Didn't you practice it then? Well, it is important to practice it again before you arrive to your fortune. You do know that if you want to achieve success on a higher level it does comes with different burdens. You have prepared for the family and friends along the way, but what about the newbies who will do anything to get close to you to destroy all that you have practice so hard for. I would like to provide you with 6 ARTs that you should practice before reaching the heights that are ahead of you.

1. **Practice the Art** of saying NO sometimes because if you find yourself saying yes to make everybody else's life better, then you will forget to continue practicing on what it will take to sustain your

success. This may be hard for some, but support is your mission, dependence is not.
2. **Practice the Art** of saying YES to new ideas because the one thing about life is that it will change. Do not ever get to comfortable believing that you cannot listen to other people's ideas, or be prepared to receive your one-way ticket back to *Ground-Zero* because you said no all the time.
3. **Practice the Art** of GIVING BACK to those who completed the journey with you. I am not talking about the along the way people because they did not make it with you for a reason. This is an important element because you want to be able to sleep sound because when you decided to take your life up a notch it started inside of you and you did not forget who helped you.
4. **Practice the Art** of Delivering Results On-Time because most often people miss golden opportunities because they procrastinate. You need to be more conscious about time than you are about money. Believe it or not, you can get more money in life, but you cannot get time back. Learn to value other peoples time because if you do not, they will not value yours. I want to talk about how important timing is,

you just may have to keep re-inventing yourself. I will talk later on in the book about how five billionaires reinvented themselves. Sometimes you will only have a window to fulfill certain opportunities and you better be prepared.

5. **Practice the Art** of STARTING OVER because believe it or not, most people do not make it to every destination they set out for. Sometimes you must change directions to reach the new desire inside of your heart. You better know that desires are what inspire true champions. Ask yourself are you a champion on the inside? The answer is, yes, and because you never forgot about the many gifts and talents you have inside of you. Many successful people have had to start over and if they still made it, so can you.

6. **Practice the Art** of GETTING OLDER, not old because you will only be as old as you feel. Practice taking care of your mind, body, and soul because if you do not take care of them, they can be a determining factor when you reach your destination. Proper nutrition/diet can add countless years on your life. Do not believe me look at most successful people as they age, follow the blueprint.

These 6 Elements can make or break your chances of sustaining success. Name that one person that you do not think highly of because he or she made it to a certain level and blew it all because of a bad choice(s). I want you to know that the goal on your journey is to prosper. How much since does it make to prepare, practice, prosper, but lose it all because of a bad choice? Remember if you prepare and practice, you can live your life in the Third Element, **Prospering**.

Element 3

Prospering while remaining well-balanced is something that is not often spoke about with convictions because for some, once they prosper, they forget. Never forget the steps, elements, the purpose, passion, or the mission because those were the things that lead you. Taking your life up a notch is a destination or an ending point, but your destination will not be complete if you do not have someone to share it with. I can tell you a sure fire way to prosper with the wrong people will lead you down a road to recovery from something. It broke my heart recently to see a man who prepared, practiced, and prospered but is now on the road to recovery. The professional basketball player Lamar Odom was an inspiration to many along-the-way while he prospered. You know now that if it can happen to him and countless others, then what will exempt you or me if we do not remain well-balanced. You should prosper with and for a purpose.

Have you dreamed of what you would do with your first million dollar check? That should be on your mind right now because you are going to make it. Prospering does not happen by accident, it requires everything and a multitude of steps to get there. As you continue to strive, I want you to take a blank check and endorse it to yourself for the amount of 1 million dollars. For those who have made their millions, you endorse a blank check to yourself and leave the amount blank because the sky is the limit for you as well. I have been fortunate to be in the presence of many Millionaires and the one question I asked them was how does it feel to have the opportunity to live your dream? Surprisingly, only 25% of them were really happy. Please do not take on the task of preparing, practicing, prospering and then realize that this is not what you wanted because sometimes if you ask for it, you just might get it. You have prospered already and probably do not realize it. There is nothing wrong with living the life that you choose to live, but please never place judgments on another person. At the end of the day, I want you to ask yourself again, do you know where you are headed?

Your destiny should be written on your face before you actually reach and achieve the mission. If a person meets you today, are you prepared to tell them where you are headed? I am not talking wholeheartedly the final destination but a projection of your path. This is important because as you know, some people that arrive in your presence might not be there to see you make it, but again, to see you fail. I heard a story that stuck with me for a long time about the greatest boxer of all times Muhammad Ali. As you know he was amongst the pioneers in the sport of boxing. He would come out to screaming fans and proceed to electrifying the crowd with his performances while he dismantled enough opponents to deserve his place in history. Winning his first boxing championship at 22 years old and by the time he retired when he was 39 years old with a record of 56 wins, 5 losses having 37 wins by way of knock outs. During one particular fight as he was being announced to enter the arena and as he proceeded he looked into the crowd and he did not notice this lady who it seemed appeared at all of his fights. He just continued to the ring and rip-to-pieces his opponents. However, before his next fight, he sent his manager to go out into the arena and see if the lady that was missing from the previous fight was in attendance. Sure enough she was and the champ decided that he would enter the arena and walk down her aisle so he could personally thank her for the support over the many years. As they announced his name he proceeded into the arena and stopped and said to the woman in his confident/assuring voice that "I would like to thank you for all of your support over the years, and I want to bring you up to the ringside to view this knockout." The woman then responded, "Over all these years you thought I was here to support you, I was only here to see you get knocked out, and I hope its tonight." The champ started laughing and preceded to the ring, nevertheless, Ali won that fight too. The moral to the story is sometimes we can become deaf to the people screaming around us. Even after you started and made your decision to prepare, practice and prosper every person will not be headed in the same direction you are. Some people will act like they are cheering but really cheering for your downfall.

Now you are ready To Make it Happen in your Life.

CHAPTER 9
Are You Ready to Make It Happen?

*"Never be afraid to try something new.
Remember amateurs built the ark.
Professionals built the Titanic."*
-Unknown-

Learning when to speak over your life and learning when to remain silent will oftentimes be the difference between winning and losing. As crazy as this may sound while preparing to make it happen, you might have to go back and start over at the beginning. When I think of the beginning it's not from day 1 of your life it's from the day you take on your Mission. Some people will have a life-long mission and some will have several missions that they may have to continuously strive for. This chapter is design to help proven professionals as well as the soon to be professionals, reach their highest achievements. The ultimate goal is to learn how to Make it Happen in your life, and for others, Making it Happen again.

I can remember when I was a young man growing up and love playing and watching basketball. I was privileged like many others to witness the greatest basketball player in the world, Michael Jordan. I saw MJ soar in the NBA for 15 seasons and change the world. He was on a mission and he did not leave until the mission was complete. For some professional basketball players making it was their mission, but for MJ, winning championships was his. I have to ask you a question, are you ready to make your dreams happen? I will provide you with **5 approaches** to making it happen.

Approach 1- *Reinvesting in others* should not seem hard to believe because I have learned that you or I can only be as great to those who we have helped along the way. Look at most successful people they contribute their success to someone other than themselves. I would like to provide you with proven professionals that have reinvested in others to continue to help them make it happen.

1. Michael Jordan- after retiring from basketball, he reinvested in other professional basketball players by becoming the majority shareholder for the Charlotte Hornets. He gave us fifteen years of us watching him succeed at his mission, now he has reinvented himself so we can now witness others.
2. Oprah Winfrey- she gave us 25 years with her Oprah Winfrey Show, since then she has bought a school in South Africa, she has assisted her friends with their own TV

shows, she has bought her own Television Network called *"OWN"* to help others, and now she has just bought stake into Weight-Watchers to help others struggling with weight.
3. Mark Zuckerberg- the CEO of Facebook has delivered a social media platform that reaches billions of people in a single day. He has now reinvested in others by donating 100 million dollars to Newark Public School System.
4. Bill Gates- has provided us with the access that operates the world, Microsoft to fulfill his mission. Now he reinvested in others by providing the Bill and Melinda Gates Foundation which is the largest philanthropist organization in the world and is committed to the eradication of malaria and polio, and controlling the spread of HIV.
5. You- The Ceo of yourself that has made a sacrifice from this day forward to seek financial freedom, and to live your purpose and reinvest in others. I believe in you and I know you too can possess the traits of the 4 above mentioned trendsetters. Are you ready to make it happen? Approach your purpose without doubt or ever thinking that it cannot happen. It's your turn now.

Approach 2- *Use someone else as inspiration* because if you have a blueprint of something that have intrigued and inspired you, you can use the philosophy to make it happen. The choice is simple, use it. I can bet you that there is a young man or girl watching and emulating their inspiration. This is why the United States of America is the greatest country to live. You can become whatever you choose to become. All you have to do is make yourself greater. In reality there is not too many things that's new under this sun. Utilize your ability to dream about the aspirations that aspirers you to help fulfill your mission. The answers are right in front of you. Are you ready to make it happen?

Approach 3- *Learn to never doubt yourself* because your age does not determine your level of success. Well if you are in your teens, mid 20's, mid 30's, mid 40's, mid 50's, mid 60's or mid-70's you too can still make it happen. It all starts with finding out what type of learning style you have. You might be a visual learner initially whereas you have to see your aspiration. Your goal at the end of your journey, you want to be a tactile/kinesthetic learner because you will want to actually feel your dreams in your soul. Your starting point was either days, weeks, months, or years ago but the mission should live on long after you are not. This will become your legacy. Remember your mission is not about you, it is about purpose.

Approach 4- *Learn how to listen to your gut* because if you or I had all of the answers then we would not need other people in the world. Keeping your ears open and your mouth closed will actually allow you to learn to give. You are now challenged to decide which do you want to become the giver or receiver? I am asking you now, are you a giver, or are you a receiver? I hope you said both because visionaries look at the world as peaks and valleys and sometimes we have to listen and receive in the peaks and become a giver in the valleys. Go to seminars, social events, and networking opportunities just to listen in the (Peaks), and then receive what you heard so you therefore, can give to others in the (Valleys). The valleys are the people who will benefit from your mission the most. Do you want to be a game-changer? This is how you change the game. Remember that having the magnitude to become a better listener will give you the ability to lead effectively. I need you to be a thinker first and a business person second. The choice is yours to win or lose because your intake is oftentimes better than what you put out.

Approach 5- *Love what you do* because a mission without the passion is not a mission, it's a job. Make your life greater than it's ever been by smiling. Keep a daily count of how many times you smile and you will be surprised at how many people will smile back at you. Only you can display what others do not see if you just share your gifts. I cannot express enough that doing anything just for money would ever be enough to fulfill what you were actually placed on this earth to do. Do you now know what you were placed on this earth to do? These approaches are given to guide your approach to making it happen in your life.

Do you know that you do not need a lot, but you have the ability to do a lot? Making it happen is not just a word, it's a place or state of being. I need you to concentrate on these 5 (W's) to help you make it happen.

- **Who-** are you targeting is one of the most important question you should ask yourself on your way to making it happen? You have already received the steps that prepared you. Your target is right in front of you and you are aiming for the center of it. You have now increased your chances of hitting a bull's-eye because you are ready to shoot. I need you to have **confidence** in yourself because you are ready to advance to the next level. The level cannot be conquered if you do not claim victory before you complete your mission.
- **What-** price are you willing to pay to uphold your character? You have to give it 200% of the times, young people often express that they are keeping it 100%. To me that mean that they are 50% coming and 50% going. I want you to be the same

coming and going. Your quest to make it happen starts with **communication** between your *will* and your *power* to make it happen. I will not say it will be easy because life is not easy. I want you to work for it so you appreciate the fruits of your labor and hard work. At this point it's not considered work anymore, it's your passion. Are you ready to live better?

- **When-** you start making it happen it will come with some backlash from others. This is your first test as a listener. I have yet to see any person fulfill his or her dream and it did not come with backlash. You have to know that it comes with the territory. But the good news is, you are built for the challenge because you **control** your actions. Controlling your actions when faced with adversity gives you the power you need to continue your passion. That is why it's so important to love what you do. You can control internal factors of your mission, but external factors are just that, out of your control. When the problems come, remember your vision is bigger than any problem. You are prepared to take your life up a notch.
- **Where-** you are now is not by accident because your life had a meaning from the beginning. I encourage you now to embrace it and walk into your destiny with a feeling of belonging. I encourage humbleness but at some point in your life

you must develop a small level of **cockiness.** The cockiness I am referring to is not to glorify what you accomplished, but a since of celebrating your achievements while on your journey. If you really want to take your life up a Notch, follow all of the desires of your heart and make it happen in your life. Where you are now cannot define where your passion will take you. Be courageous enough to believe that your best is yet to come.

- **Why-** understanding why you were chosen to make it happen is a core/foundation course in your life. You have already past all of the prerequisites. You are chosen and you are ready to take your life up a notch. If you are still wondering, why me, because of **coolness.** Yes, you are going to make it happen and look cool while doing it. Yes, you have coolness associated with your passion. Tell me if you know any successful person that you admire that's not cool. Your coolness is something you need because sometimes when you are the leader, you need to be able to put out fires. Ask yourself, do you want to be cool.

Life has shown me many things, and I have ventured off into different careers but I finally understand my mission, it's to Motivate. I want to express my deepest gratitude to you for taking the time to read this book because without you I am nothing. I want you to know that from this day forth, I am standing in solidarity behind YOU to make it happen in your life. If at any time you need a reminder of how to take your life up a notch? Just remember that the sky is the limit for YOU and no one can stop it.

> "Only two things come out of the choices we make in life, benefits and consequences."
> -Ernest D. Sullivan-

You need your next choice to be beneficial for you and the ones that believe in you the most. Take a bow because you have successfully made it to the airport; now look at your accomplishments thus far. You received your boarding pass/mission, checked in your baggage/goals, walked through the security check points; you can breathe easy and just fly. Do you know that you bypassed haters and naysayers, now you are on the plane on your way to the Sky Is The Limit Boulevard. Let me be the person again to tell you welcome aboard!

CHAPTER 10
The Sky is the Limit for YOU!

"No boundary or barrier surrounds the heart of a person that loves their self and others."
-Shannon L. Alder-

Now that you are seated on the plane you can now begin to release all that is inside of you. Just to think you started from ground-zero and you will now see life from a different view. Start imagining it being a sunny day while you are traveling to success. You have been through enough clouds in your life. Now, believe that your success is yet to come. You now understand that fame is only driven by the weak but your mission is far greater. Most people when they travel they book a round trip ticket, but you are ambitious and courageous enough to have bought a one-way ticket to success. Remembering that fame only lasting for a moment will keep you humble enough to stay focused. I congratulate you now because knowing that you have risen above all obstacles that have come upon your life and you are now ready to move higher to life's hemisphere.

TAKING YOUR LIFE UP A NOTCH
"The Sky Is The Limit For You"

The power you possess was not given to you only through reading books, listening to others, or even by accident. The power has always been inside of you. Your power is different from any other person on this planet and now you get to show the world how strong mentally, physically, and spiritually you are. The view looks great from this point and just to think for some your plane just took off and for others yours are about to soar higher. It may have taken some of us a while to realize that the sky is the limit but after surveying our gifts and talents we could have believed it all the time. At this view point, you are not having any regrets because you are now driven by a powerful image inside of your head. Some people are driven solely on what's based on their hearts and beliefs, but in reality it all started in their mind. Your mind still imagines, but you are now at a vantage point to follow your mission because your mind is where the dreams were started and developed. Remember after learning from your past of wild experiences, hurt, pain, envy, jealousness, strife, resentment, dilutions, set-backs, head-aches, do not forget you hidden them in rooms inside of your brain. Now I want you to think about the times that you were happy, loving, caring, accepting, understanding, polite, ambitious, open-minded, and even in love because from this point forward, you will be following your destiny. One last reality check is, do not forget to lock the doors to negativity. When you are traveling to success, all of your negative thoughts cannot be reinforced at any point on this journey. Do not let anything, I mean nothing poison your thoughts before the doors swing open to your success. If you do not believe it, you cannot achieve it. You belong on this flight now be ready for greatness.

Your mission comes with a stamp and copyright that starts from this day forward with a dash with no end date. You are the only one who can end your mission because it belongs to you. Please do not make the mistake I made and start a mission with others and they ended it without my stamp or copyright of approval. I truly understood the mission and believed in it, but now, I give myself assurance that my next mission will be mines alone. Do not leave your mission in the hands of someone else because they might take control of the plane you are on and reroute your mission. Tell yourself now that your mission is on, and that you will be the only person that will have total control over it. By the way, I am now the passenger sitting next to you while you are on your way to taking your life up a notch.

Your decision to take your life up a notch will not be in vain because if you never get on the plane, how would you ever know if the sky is the limit. You can look at your life as if being in an Olympic Relay Race, just think you never knew when the baton would be passed to you in the past. I am excited to tell you that you can see the person/mission coming to you next. This plane ride in your mind is how you begin to take your life up a notch. This is how you are getting ready for the baton to be passed. I am appreciating flying next to you because this is when you can reflect on all the times you attempted to be great and failed. Also, it can help you reflect on the many set-backs you encountered before you got here. In addition, this could be a reminder of who wronged you, held you back, and did not believe you even when you did not believe in yourself. I am glad you received your receipt that was engraved with the words, paid in full, for your one-way ticket to success. No one but you will ever know the entire price you had to pay because of those bedrooms you had to lock and unlock. This should be confirmation to all that belongs on this journey, and you are not traveling on a stand-by ticket. Your seat on this plane is guaranteed and you cannot be bumped by any other passengers. You can now sit back comfortably from this day forward and know that the sky is the limit for you.

If you have ever flown on an airplane the pilot will interrupt all transmissions and give an announcement about the conditions ahead and how long it will be before the plane lands. Never get discouraged on your way to The Sky is the Limit Boulevard because some flights are connecting flights. That means maybe they have conditions and circumstances that may cause the plane you are on to land and to take off again.

Imagine these as the conditions and circumstances, which they are letting passengers off at their journey point. The plane may be picking up other success seekers to continue on the flight with you. Now you can start to remember the relay race and start saying my journey had begun. We live in a huge world and we have domestic and international flights. Your dream may be so huge that it may need to be shared all across the world. Now that you are taking your life up a notch this is really important to know where you want your final destination to end. I can feel how strong you have become because you are sitting right next to me. Your strength combined with my strength will produce POWER. This can open up doors for both of us. And we can have the Sky is Limit Boulevard as our destination together. It's time now to believe it without any doubt that we will make it. Put it in your heart today.

The doors will open for you and I know you are ready. That's why you must have a destination for your heart to follow. While on this plane understand once you accomplish your mission after landing, eventually you will have to follow your heart and know where you are headed again. Knowing where you are headed again is the easy part for some people, but you and I may still be focused on our first mission.

My next book will talk about **The Fight to Stay on Top** before you have to move. Your itinerary should have a landing airport where your mission lies. I am glad to know that you are not nervous while traveling with me because a certain sense of calmness is a must on any aircraft. After certain situations, passengers cannot start on a journey and forget about all the preparation it took to board this flight. Do you remember I gave examples of how some people prepare, practice for greatness, and prosper, then make a bad choice, and had to return back to ground-zero? Never forget after you make it to The Sky is the Limit Boulevard, we can suffer a setback sometimes by the acts of others. What do you know? Here goes the pilot again interrupting your opportunity to reflect while on your way to your destination? This time he is announcing that this is your landing place. It's a term that's used when a plane lands and it's called "wheels-down." Do you know what time it is now? It's time to make it happen in your life.

This is the most important part of your mission and you can never take this for granted. It's making it happen in your life. Now I have mentioned that YOU and others have to follow certain steps to make it happen, but ultimately it's not about YOU, it's about the mission. When you begin to live your passion that is when you are making it happen and not a moment before. I gave several processes, steps, ways, phases, elements and I have a little more to give you to have the complete foundation to get you to your mission. Making it happen is now your responsibility because you have people that are now depending on you. We talked about all people we possibly left behind, but now you have to make it happen for all the people who took the journey with you. You will only be as great to those that you help, impact, and affect positively, while making it happen. Now ask yourself again, are you ready to make it happen?

While you are making your dreams a reality, you are required to do a few things, and these things are both regular and irregular.

- Keep a smile on your face at all times because the minute you are not enjoying what you are doing, then you cannot affectively make it happen.
- Associate your mission only with people that will increase your ability to make it happen. If you do not imagine ground-zero.
- Give 1000% every day because you paid a price to get where you are, and where you are going and it does come with added responsibilities. It will be times when you will have to pursue your passion by going to work when you do not feel good. Do you know the saying, "sometimes you have to do whatever you have to do, to make it happen?"
- Do something you always dreamed of doing because at the end of the day you

only have one life to live. Remember, the sky is the limit for you.
- Make the life of someone else better because then you can earn a place in history that many people before you and after you missed, that will be your legacy.

This has been a great ride and I appreciate being the chosen vessels to deliver the good news. This world is filled with opportunities and only the person(s) that believes success can achieve it. The time is now to accept your gift and when you begin to see your dreams come true, pull out another talent because it's inside you. I want you to continue to believe in yourself and start your journey today. **Take your Life UP a Notch** because **The Sky is the Limit for you**.

-Ernest D. Sullivan-
Thank You!

THE MOTIVATING MOMENTS

1. Can you remember a moment when you were at your lowest and something or someone gave you what you needed, that was not by accident, and it was confirmation that your life has meaning? You are worth more than money can buy.
2. Do you find winning to be a bad thing? If so, watch how losing affect even the people you think have it all? Choose to win because you are a winner.
3. Have you ever had someone to rip some money/currency from your hand and it tore? Do you know I have seen money washed with cloths, stepped on, crumbled up, even covered in blood, but the powerful thing about it, it still has value. Some people have endured a lot worse and still succeeded. Guess what, your life has value, also.
4. When was the last time you needed help and no one was around to help you, what happened? Do not answer because you did not need them as much as you thought because you are still here. Learn

to stop worrying about things that you do not have control over. It's just life.

5. A week ago, I saw a man with one leg struggling to get from point A to Point B, then the next day I saw a woman with one arm trying to fasten her jacket. Do you know they both accomplished their task? What is your excuse? You can do anything you set your mind to do. Quitting is never an option.

6. What is your idea of the perfect family, a husband, a wife, ex, amount of children and family pet? You can still believe that because no matter what situation you are in now, some one can come into your life and complete your family.

7. Do you know things can make a difference in your life just like people can make a difference in your life? Example of things, Education, Attitude, Health, Wealth, and even a simple Smile.

8. If you do not think you have made any progress over the last five years, go to a funeral home near you and ask to see the registry. You have come further along in life then many. Be thankful you have an opportunity to keep making progress.

9. Have you ever asked yourself what is your favorite time of the day? Me either

because every day above ground means we have a little time left to enjoy our life.

What if I told you that there was a man that some people have met but many have never met, but that man has mad love for YOU? There is no motivation in this question because that man is me. I love each and every one of you.

–**Ernest D. Sullivan**-

10 Reasons Why You……

1. Should be happy is because smiling is better than crying.

2. Should love every human that walks the earth because all lives matters.

3. Should live in the neighborhood that you reside in, be a positive influence, and make a difference.

4. Should go back to school again, so your children's, children will know they came from greatness.

5. Should take advantage of every opportunity that comes before you, because if you do not someone else will.

6. Should commit to walking, jogging, and running, because you want to live a productive life without limitations.

7. Should plan a trip that you dreamed about but never imagined going, because this year change is coming in your life.

8. Should help at least 1 person a week without accepting anything in return

because maybe that will be your down payment when you need help.

9. Should listen to someone other than yourself because just maybe they may have something important to say.

10. Should sing with your loud voice the alphabets backwards, I mean literally. I will sing with you Z, Y, X, W, and V. We can stop now because this book has brought me that much closer to YOU.

Notes To Start Your Engine

-----------------------------------To be a sponsor to spread the word that it's worth Taking Your Life Up A Notch because The Sky is the Limit for YOU!

Donate a Book

Please contact us at ernestsullivan3@gmail.com for further instructions.

Donations for book orders should be made payable to: Ernest D. Sullivan Enterprise

Only Certified Checks or Money Orders are accepted!

BE A SPONSOR!

Give back by partnering with Ernest D. Sullivan Enterprises. Become a sponsor and support us by participating in our "Donate a Book Campaign!" Your donation can be life changing for future leaders who need the motivation of this book. By purchasing the book, *Taking Your Life Up A Notch, The Sky Is The Limit For You* for the price of $16.95 plus $5.25 for shipping and handling, you can make a difference by donating a book or a box of books to men and women in prison, church ministries, schools, homeless shelters, loved ones across the world, or just to family members. You make the choice and we can help change the world.

All partners or sponsors will receive a free gift

courtesy of Mr. Ernest D. Sullivan

with orders of 25 Books or more!

About the Author
Ernest D. Sullivan

ABOUT THE AUTHOR/Motivational Speaker

"Only two things come out of the choices a person makes in their lives, Benefits and Consequences."

Ernest "The Future" Sullivan a renowned Motivational Speaker, Mentor, Life Coach, Consultant, Professional Development Trainer and the Author of the book titled, *Life is About Choices*! Has over 17 years of service in Public Speaking, Healthcare, Marketing, Business Development, and Higher Education.

Memorable Accomplishments:
- **Key Note Motivational Speaker Robert at Covington Philadelphia 76ers Youth Camp July 2016**
- **Key Note Commencement Stagg Elementary School June 2016**
- **Stage Bill "The Black Social Network" Morehouse College September 2015**
- **Key Note Commencement Speaker at Computer System Institute Graduation December of 2014**
- **Key Note Commencement Speaker at Robert Morris University Graduation November of 2008**
- **Distinguished Alumni Award Recipient of Robert Morris University for 2008**

A Graduate of Robert Morris University, **MBA**

SPECIAL THANKS

I would like to give special acknowledgments to the following individuals who have supported me over the years and pushed me to do all things that are before me.

Special Thanks: To my wife Katrina Sullivan thanks for everything that you have done for me.

Special Thanks: My sisters, Casandra Travis, and Jamie Johnson.

Special Thanks to my cousins: Bruce Sullivan, Dion Siler, John Sullivan, Michael Sullivan, Dushon Decker, Jamie Siler, Kevin Hunter Jr., Harold Darnell Siler (Deceased) and Eric Maurice Brunson (Deceased) Kordero Hunter (Deceased) (MVP Foundation).

Sharon Sullivan, Bridget Tomlinson, Kim Hunter, Shelee Morris-Butler, Antoinette Sullivan, Quintina Smith, Falon Sullivan, and Erica Sullivan.

Special Thanks: My future leaders of tomorrow.

To the entire LeClaire Courts Housing Projects, Divine Entertainment.

To my brothers from another mother: Anthony Allen, Darron Randle, Lou Parks, Lavelle Williams, Robert Smith, Maine Williams, Svengali

Banks, and My M.O.B. family. This is where my journey began; I want to say thank you all.

There has been many more family and friends that deserve acknowledgment, so I want to celebrate you as well.

I THANK YOU ALL
-Ernest D. Sullivan-

www.ingramcontent.com/pod-product-compliance
Lightning Source LLC
Chambersburg PA
CBHW070615010526
44118CB00012B/1520